I0295828

INDIAN TALES OF THE RAJ

To my grandparents,
from whom I could have learned so much more

ZAREER MASANI

INDIAN TALES OF THE RAJ

HALL GREEN COLLEGE

954.035

29962

LIBRARY AND RESOURCES

BBC BOOKS

Map by Line and Line

Published by BBC Books,
A division of BBC Enterprises Ltd,
Woodlands, 80 Wood Lane,
London W12 0TT

First published 1987

© Zareer Masani 1987

ISBN 0 563 20528 8

Typeset in 10/11½ Sabon by Wilmaset, Birkenhead, Wirral
Printed in England by St Edmundsbury Press Ltd,
Bury St Edmunds, Suffolk

CONTENTS

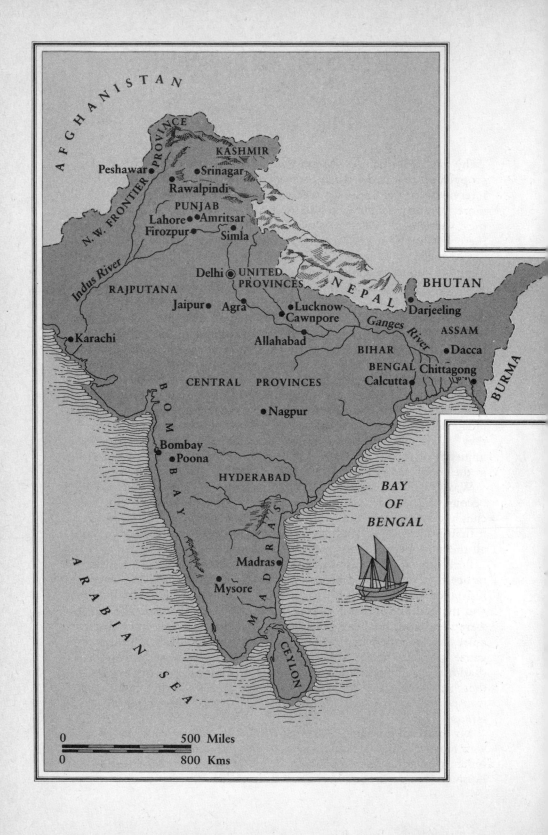

AFGHANISTAN

KASHMIR

Peshawar
Srinagar

Rawalpindi

N. W. FRONTIER PROVINCE

PUNJAB
Lahore Amritsar
Firozpur Simla

Delhi UNITED
PROVINCES

BHUTAN

NEPAL

RAJPUTANA

Jaipur Agra Lucknow
Cawnpore

Darjeeling

Ganges River

ASSAM

Karachi

Allahabad

BIHAR

Dacca

Indus River

BENGAL

Chittagong

Calcutta

BURMA

CENTRAL PROVINCES

Nagpur

B
O
M
B
A
Y

Bombay
Poona

HYDERABAD

BAY
OF
BENGAL

ARABIAN SEA

M
A
D
R
A
S

Madras

Mysore

CEYLON

| 0 | 500 Miles |
| 0 | 800 Kms |

ANCESTRAL VOICES

'Why are the British so obsessed with the Raj?' was a question which cropped up repeatedly when I travelled round India last year, recording interviews for the Radio 4 series, *Indian Tales of the Raj.* I interviewed more than fifty people who had lived and worked with the British when they were there. Once awakened, their memories were prolific; but there was little trace of nostalgia, none of the yearning for the good old days which one is so used to hearing from British 'survivors'. Instead, there was polite bewilderment that anyone should be interested in the Raj almost four decades after it ended.

A couple of Indian 'survivors' were less than polite, like 83-year-old J. R. D. Tata, head of India's most cosmopolitan and patrician business dynasty, who flatly refused to record his memories of a humiliating colonial past. Another reluctant aristocrat was Lady Ranu Mukherji, wealthy doyenne of the Calcutta arts world, who is believed by some to have been the prototype for Paul Scott's Lady Chatterji. She made it clear that she was too busy arranging a local exhibition to spare any time for the Raj. Some of my own contemporaries of the post-independence generation were even more negative – shouldn't the BBC, they asked, be examining instead the far more invasive American influence of today; or better still, looking ahead to India's own arrival in the computer age?

Was I, after all, conjuring up the ghosts of a vanished era that had become irrelevant outside the pages of British fiction? My own childhood memories told me otherwise. The Raj I inherited had more to it than princes, tigers and mem-sahibs in distress; and its legacies were all the more pervasive for being so easily taken for granted.

Born three months after independence, I had grown up in a family, or rather two families, as proud of their services to empire as of their resistance to it. Some of my earliest memories were of my grandparents and the bedtime stories I coaxed and cajoled out of them. The stories were their own, not read from books; and they were an entertainment more avidly anticipated and consumed than any since. Through my gauze mosquito-net in a darkened room, all I saw were faceless, grey shadows, caught occasionally in the light of an open doorway. But in that nebulous hour between wakefulness and sleep, their voices transported me to a world where history was often stranger than fantasy.

My maternal grandmother, in particular, seemed to epitomise all that was most dashing and glamorous about the family's past: the only Indian woman to drive a phaeton, at full tilt, through the streets of old Kanpur (or Cawnpore, as the British called it); the first to make speeches in the legislature of the then United Provinces;[1] and the first in the province to dance with a British governor.

Life for her, I learned as I grew older, had not always been easy. A north Indian Hindu of the *Kayasth* or scribe caste, she had married at fourteen the eldest son of a destitute landowner who had gambled away his wealth. In a remarkably audacious change of lifestyle and career, my grandfather, then sixteen, had decided to restore the family fortunes by training as a textile engineer in Manchester. He sailed for England, and my grandmother, only fifteen, went with him.

Life in Edwardian England cannot have been easy for a shy, teenaged, Indian wife who spoke no English. But in later years, she made light of her difficulties and laughed about how she drove her English teacher to distraction by insisting on 'soap' at table and 'soup' in the bathroom.

When they returned from England to the northern industrial centre of Kanpur, my grandfather's new, Western qualifications, coupled with hard work and a shrewd business acumen, worked like a magic wand. Starting as a technician in the British-owned New Victoria Textile Mill, he was successful enough to buy out its British proprietor within a decade. Making skilful use of the colonial managing agency system and the tax concessions offered by the princely states,[2] he went on to establish a chain of other family-owned companies across northern India. From business to politics was a small step for him; but unlike other Indian industrialists of his generation, he was an ardent empire loyalist till the bitter end. As an Executive Councillor, or member of the viceregal cabinet, in the 1940s, his opposition to Indian nationalism was hawkish even by British standards; and the Raj rewarded his loyalty with three separate orders of knighthood.

He died before I was old enough to remember him; but a silver-framed, full-length portrait of him still graces my mother's drawing-room, his bespectacled, pugnacious, brown face glaring defiantly from the eighteenth-century ceremonial garb of a viceregal councillor – buckled shoes, white hose and knee-breeches, a gold-braided tail-coat glittering with medals, a ceremonial sword by his side, and a plumed hat under his arm. Led on by such glittering prizes, my mother's parents dined and danced with the British and organised grand tiger-shoots for them; and the children graduated from a British governess to British schools and universities. But by the standards of the far more westernised metropolis of Bombay, where I grew up, they still seemed strongly rooted in a feudal, north Indian culture – equally at home in Urdu and English, connoisseurs of Indian classical music and dance, though fond of Western theatre and ballet. They were practising though not orthodox Hindus, who celebrated

1 Now UP or Uttar Pradesh, India's largest and most populous state, in the northern, Hindi-speaking heartland.
2 India's nearly six hundred princely or native states covered roughly a third of the sub-continent. Though under the paramountcy of the British Crown, they were on a different constitutional footing from British India proper and enjoyed a fair measure of autonomy in fiscal and other administrative matters. After the British left, the states were integrated into independent India and Pakistan.

festivals like *Diwali* and *Holi*[1] with as much enthusiasm as Christmas. Their meals seemed to sum up their eclecticism – rich *Mughlai*[2] food at lunch, eaten with the hands off traditional silver *thalis*, and Anglo-Indian roasts and soufflés for dinner.

My father's family, Bombay Parsis,[3] were a rather different kettle of fish. By the time I knew them, they might almost have been British-born, and indeed prided themselves on being temperamentally more 'Anglo-Saxon' than Indian. But curiously enough, their very anglicism made them politically far less loyal to the British than my maternal relatives. This was because their particular brand of westernisation owed much less to Anglo-Indian social fashions than to an austere Victorian ethic which stressed integrity, hard work and discipline and shunned the more ostentatious and hedonistic revelry of the Raj. My paternal grandfather was the first Indian to become Municipal Commissioner of Bombay and Vice-Chancellor of its university; but his leisure hours were spent, not socialising with the British, but on philanthropic endowments and on the writing of scholarly historical and anthropological works. Although he decided that it would be churlish to refuse the knighthood that the Raj conferred on him, he promptly hid it away in a drawer and preferred to be known as plain 'Mr'.

My parents had grown up in the inter-war decades, when the nationalist movement was reaching its peak, and their tales of the Raj were about youthful rebellion rather than the glories of empire. My father could look back on a long career of civil disobedience and imprisonment, starting in 1932. My grandfather ordered him out of the house for his socialist activities; but father and son had continued to meet once a week for lunch, when my grandfather supplemented the meagre rations of a full-time political activist with a good meal at Bombay's Grand Hotel. My mother, too, had stories of her student days during the Quit India movement of the 1940s, when her sisters and she smuggled confidential information from her father's official files to the Congress underground and shouted anti-British slogans when the Viceroy came to dinner. My parents' elopement itself caused something of a sensation in 1945, not only because inter-marriage between different communities was still rare, but because the daughter of such a die-hard loyalist was marrying a prominent nationalist.

When I appeared on the scene two years later, the British had left; and both generations of my elders – nationalist parents and loyalist grandparents – seemed to miss the romance and adventure of times past. British rituals lingered on in our home. My parents spoke only English to each other and to me, and followed British social etiquette down to the last crease in the damask napkins at their dinner-table. Most of our servants had worked for British masters and addressed their new

1 *Diwali* is the Festival of Lights which marks the Hindu New Year, and *Holi* is the colourful Hindu festival of spring.
2 The north Indian cuisine which originated in the Mughal courts.
3 India's smallest and most westernised minority, the Parsis were eighth-century migrants from pre-Islamic Persia.

employers as 'Sahib' and 'Mem-Sahib'; I was 'Baba'. I particularly remember our impressive, mustachioed butler, a north Indian Muslim, whom my mother triumphantly brought back with her after one of her visits to her parental home. He had spent his youth as valet to a British ICS officer, who had retired in England, but with whom he still corresponded regularly. Since the Sahib wrote in English, which Nanhey Khan, as he was called, could neither read nor write, I acted as his translator and scribe. I was to find his tales of serving the sahibs almost as inventive and enticing as the cooking of his British-trained brother, who later joined the household as our cook and produced every winter the best Christmas pudding I have ever eaten.

All that, of course, was a long time ago in the 1950s; and my family belonged to a tiny minority – a few thousand among several hundred millions. But it says a great deal about independent India that we never felt we were the odd ones out. I went to school with children who either came from a similar background or wished they had. It was an Anglican school, whose principal was an elderly, red-faced Englishman with a machine-gun stutter, appropriately named Mr Gunnery. The teachers were mostly younger Britons or 'Anglo-Indians' (in the sense of mixed race). We affluent Indians looked down upon the racially hybrid 'Anglos', as we called them; but we adopted more of their values than we realised.

At morning assembly, we sang British hymns, chanted the Lord's Prayer and heard prefects reading the lesson for the day from the Bible. In the classroom, we prided ourselves on being good at English literature and history and scorned the Indian languages which had been made compulsory by government decree. In some ways, we were even less Indian than our parents, who had grown up under the Raj. My mother took her Master's degree in English literature, and she dined, danced and played golf with the British at Bombay's exclusive Willingdon Club. But she had also studied Sanskrit and Urdu and trained in classical Indian dance. Resistance to Anglo-Indian culture was clearly stronger when Indians were still fighting British rule.

Schools like mine are still crucial stepping-stones to the more select colleges founded during the Raj. When we of the convent schools, as Indians call them, arrived at university, we had to rub shoulders with a still-silent majority from the Indian-medium or vernacular schools, of whose very existence we had been scarcely aware. But with English as the medium of instruction, we were still the chosen few. We dominated the lecture-rooms, the debating societies, college plays and magazines, and became the favourites of the lecturers, some of whom had British degrees. As for the 'vernaculars', as we contemptuously labelled them, we made fun of their Indian English and their orthodox ways. And when, against all odds, they sometimes beat us at examinations, we did not really care. We knew we would still fare better in the job stakes and in admissions to the British or American universities on which we had set our sights.

Those of us who did make it to Oxbridge often found it a rude awakening. We discovered how the children of the old Anglo-India must have felt when they arrived after long absence in the mother-country. Our picture of Britain was received from parents and teachers who had studied there thirty years ago. And so we had to start afresh, discarding our hopelessly old-fashioned tweeds and conventions for the Beatlemania of the Sixties. Since then, the arrival of American film and television culture in India has narrowed the time-lag between the fashions of its upper class and those of the West. But the power of that class and the gulf that divides it from other Indians is, if anything, wider.

Reflecting on this growing gap between India's rich and poor, between the ostentatious, five-star luxury of the urban élite and the crisis of rural unemployment and landlessness, prominent political scientists and development economists have discerned in independent India a new colonial domination of the urban centres, where wealth and decision-making are concentrated, over their rural hinterland. If there is a new internal colonialism, Indians of my generation and class are undoubtedly its guardians – captains of its industry and professions, editors of its newspapers and other media, and front-men for its political parties. And for us the Raj still has a relevance, not merely because we are its legacy, but because we have lost what was best in our colonial heritage: the idealism and courage, scholarship and versatility of an older generation which accepted the challenge of the West without being conquered by it.

The experience of that generation of Indians could also be a long-awaited antidote to the Western Raj-mania which many Indians find so irksome. One of the most galling legacies of empire is that its story has so far been told almost entirely by the former colonial rulers. The understandable nostalgia of British 'survivors', confined to Cheltenham and Tunbridge Wells after the wide, open spaces where they ruled the destinies of millions, has inevitably coloured contemporary British perceptions of the Raj, turning it into a sort of equivalent of the American Wild West. In this mythical, imperial frontier, with its swashbuckling heroes, lost jewels and far pavilions, Indians themselves have tended to dwindle into colourful but insignificant specks on an exotic landscape, figuring either as opulent and scheming potentates or as noble savages tamed into loyal soldiers and servants.

The British, it is sometimes said, have never paid much heed to what other races think of them; and this was one of their greatest weaknesses in the heyday of empire. But perhaps the time has come when they can begin to see themselves as Indians saw them; not the princes they propped up or the servants they commanded, but the Indians who have been the most enduring legacy of the Raj – the Western-educated middle class whom the British fostered to serve their interests, but which eventually threw them out.

The tales which follow are told by Indians from many different walks of life – former civil servants, army officers, businessmen, politicians, lawyers, teachers, journalists and artists – a cross-section of the many thousands who worked for the British, made friends with them, and learned to do without them. Rooted in an ancient civilisation of their own, and yet the most anglicised, and often anglophile, of Britain's former colonial subjects, they are peculiarly well equipped to assess the

Raj and its legacies. Their perspective is certainly different from that of British 'survivors', but their memories and feelings are no more uniform or homogeneous than India itself. Their voices range across the spectrum from fond admiration to bitter resentment; and I have tried, as far as possible, to let them speak for themselves without interference. The last truly colonial generation of Indians is starting to die out, and I hope this book has recorded some of their wisdom before it is too late.

SERVING THE SAHIBS
BEARERS OF THE CANOPY

> *Everywhere the British presence, even though unseen, was not*
> *unfelt. If you were posted to a small district, for example, there was*
> *probably no British officer there at all. But you were conscious all*
> *the time that you were part of the British Raj. It was like a kind of*
> *overall canopy or a cloud over your head all the time.*
>
> Rajeshwar Dayal (Indian Civil Service – Retired)

For over a century, the British ruled, directly or indirectly, over most of the Indian sub-continent. And yet, throughout this period, which ended with independence in 1947, the actual number of Britons in India was tiny. It touched its peak at the turn of the century at about 100,000 and then went into a decline as independence drew nearer. Even at its peak, the entire British presence in India could have been squeezed into a football stadium; and it was spread over a vast sub-continent with a rapidly increasing population of more than 300 millions.

This numerical fact makes the relatively stable survival of the Raj for so long a period a remarkable colonial achievement. The secret of its success was that the British in India chose to colonise people and minds rather than territory. And the results, whether in administration, law or education, proved far more enduring and pervasive than any policy of white settlement could have been.

The channel for this colonisation was India's existing political and administrative élite. The early British conquerors annexed Indian kingdoms and dethroned their rulers; but they took over almost intact their administrative systems and cadres. This was because the British were essentially traders, serving the East India Company, for whom territorial control was subordinate to commercial profits. Their pragmatism was possible because India was unique among Britain's colonial possessions in having developed, long before its conquest, an administrative hierarchy which extended, at least in theory, from an imperial centre down to the district level.

Although the Raj claimed the credit for India's political unification, the sub-continent had a geo-political unity that dated back 2000 years before the British conquest to the Hindu-Buddhist Mauryan empire. The Maurya emperors had united most of the sub-continent under their rule between the fourth and second centuries BC; and their imperial ideal was echoed from the fourth to sixth centuries AD by a later Hindu dynasty, the Guptas, and more recently by the Mughal empire established in the sixteenth century.

The Mughals (derived from 'Mongol') had led the last of several waves of Central Asian invaders who had overrun northern India during the medieval period. Despite their external origins and Islamic faith, they had assimilated rapidly into Hindu India and established a monarchy that was every bit as 'national' and centralised as that of their British contemporaries, the Tudors. It had lasted two hundred years; and its decline in the eighteenth century left a political vacuum which the British were quick to fill.

The East India Company always maintained that empire was thrust upon it by the need to protect its trade, as Mughal authority disintegrated into anarchy with the rise of individual warlords. But the Mughal dynasty continued to command a peculiar reverence across the sub-continent long after it had lost effective power. The East India Company itself began its imperial career in 1765 as the *Diwan* or Revenue Minister of the Mughal Emperor for the province of Bengal, and accepted a nominal form of Mughal suzerainty until the Mutiny of 1857.

Though it began as a mutiny by the Indian sepoys or soldiers of the Company's Bengal Army, the revolt of 1857 expanded into a last-ditch battle by traditional India to ward off growing colonial interference with its religious customs and feudal pride. It found a national figurehead in the last Mughal emperor, by then a virtual prisoner of the East India Company, round whom the rebellious sepoys rallied. But the fall of the Mughal capital, Delhi, and the capture and execution by the British of most of the imperial family, marked the end of Mughal India. The British Crown took over from the Company; Queen Victoria assumed the imperial mantle; and the Raj proper began. Indian nationalism would have to await new champions among the rising middle classes, who were as yet the most loyal servants of the new colonial order.

The role of Indians in the higher levels of the East India Company's administration had a chequered history. Under the first British Governor-General, Warren Hastings (1772–85), they kept their existing high offices under new masters. But Hastings's successor, Lord Cornwallis (1786–93), reserved all senior posts for the Company's British officials in the name of reducing corruption and nepotism. The basic unit of administration, however, remained the ancient Indian district or *taluka*, first created by the Mauryan emperors two centuries before Christ, and later inherited by the Mughals and the British. The subordinate ranks of administration remained entirely Indian, and their main function continued to be the collection of land revenue. The only difference was that they were recruited increasingly on a competitive rather than hereditary basis.

The ban on Indians holding senior posts was officially dropped in 1833, when an Act of Parliament promised that race would no longer be a disqualification for the highest posts in the Company's service; and this was reiterated in Queen Victoria's proclamation of 1858, when the Crown took over from the Company. In practice, however, the Indian Civil Service or ICS, which was set up to fill these posts, remained outside the reach of Indians till after the First World War. Recruitment to the service was by competitive examination held in London in the English language, and there was an age limit of nineteen. The number of Indians who could meet these qualifications was tiny, and the few who succeeded in gaining entry were weeded out by more overt prejudice.

And yet it was only a matter of time before the thousands of Indians who were graduating from the new universities and who supplied the lower ranks of British Indian administration would demand and secure access to the senior levels. The political reforms reluctantly conceded by the Raj in 1919 opened the doors; and in 1923 arrangements were made for the ICS examination to be held simultaneously in England and India. The Raj set itself the target of a service which would be half Indian and half British; and during the next two decades there was rapid progress towards that goal.

Nevertheless, old attitudes died hard; and many British officers resented Indianisation till the bitter end, though they were usually too polite to say so openly. Rajeshwar Dayal, who retired as independent India's Foreign Secretary, joined the ICS in the 1930s, when Indianisation was well under way. 'I'm not quite sure that our British colleagues entirely accepted us,' he says. 'I think they would have been happy if it had remained an all-British service. For instance, certain districts which were supposed to be rather better than others were more or less reserved for British officers.' Another retired ICS veteran, Dharam Vir, got the same impression. 'There was always the background of a feeling,' he says, 'that the Indian element was there more because of compulsion than for any other reason.'

Hostility to Indianisation was far more open among the non-official European community; and it focused particularly on the fact that the entry of Indians into the judicial branch of the service spelled the end of the privileged legal status which Europeans had enjoyed as the ruling race. Prejudice was particularly strong in a planters' province like Assam in the north-east, where an Indian district officer was still a rarity until after independence. Nari Rustamji, the first Indian to be given charge of the Dibrugarth tea-district in Assam, acknowledges that he was only acceptable to the plantocracy because he was then far more British than Indian, having been to school and university in England, where his parents had settled. Even so, he was mistaken for a travelling salesman when he arrived on the doorstep of the Chief Secretary of Assam at the start of his ICS career.

I arrived in Shillong, which was the capital of Assam in those days, with practically no money at all. There was some mismanagement in our financial affairs, and so I couldn't take a taxi to go to the Chief Secretary's house. I had been invited to stay with the Chief Secretary. And so I picked up a couple of porters, and I had a violin and a viola which I carried myself. I walked up to the Chief Secretary's house with these porters carrying my bedding and two boxes. One was a tin box of books and another was a leather trunk with my clothes. I rang the bell and waited in the verandah. After a little time, I heard some steps in the passage, and the door was opened. And this lady, a European, she looked at me, she looked me up and down, looked at my viola and looked at my violin, looked at these porters with the baggage, and said: 'Thank you very much. Nothing this afternoon. Thank you very much indeed.' I had to convince her that I wasn't a travelling salesman. She was all kindness when she realised that I was the young Assistant Commissioner who was coming to stay with her. She took me in, lit the fire and gave me a very good tea.

For most Indians of the new, professional middle class, entry to the exclusive ICS, known half-seriously as the 'Heavenborn', became the pinnacle of achievement, an opportunity to join the colonial equivalent of the Hindu Brahmin caste. Many parents built their children's education, and sometimes their own lives, around this supreme ambition. Nari Rustamji's parents, for example, uprooted themselves from their native city of Lahore in Punjab and settled in a provincial English city so that their two sons could go to a British public school and improve their prospects for the ICS examination. Rustamji remembers how he was groomed for the service by his British headmaster, himself a retired ICS officer.

He had a real feel for India. He studied Sanskrit; he loved talking about India, told us stories about his work in India. I think he felt that it was a means of keeping up his connection with India, of which he was so very fond. He was a classical scholar, and I think he rather thought of India in terms of the Roman Empire – the proconsuls and so forth – people going out and governing India. His main object really was that I should get a classical scholarship to Cambridge. And so his whole concentration was on the Classics: Latin, Greek, ancient history and ancient philosophy, with no science, no chemistry, no economics.

This classical education was designed to create colonial rulers who would emulate Plato's philosopher-king. But, as Rustamji confesses, the absence of economics and other modern disciplines was a disadvantage which became particularly obvious after independence.

The training of Indian recruits, once they passed the ICS examination, was intended to ensure that they became as far as possible replicas of their British colleagues. They spent a probationary year at Oxford or Cambridge, where they were expected to acquire a smattering of history, law and languages, but more importantly, says Rajeshwar Dayal, to become good horsemen and pick up British social graces.

What they expected was that we should be good all-rounders, people who could get on horseback and ride around the country, meting out perhaps rough and ready justice and inspiring confidence. The old spirit of the empire-builders was still very much alive, and we were expected, somewhat vicariously, to uphold the White Man's Burden of empire. So they were looking for the sort of qualities that they themselves favoured in their public schools. If you didn't make the grade – being a good all-rounder, good with the gun, good on horseback – then you were consigned to the judiciary, which wasn't regarded as a very glorious career in those days. Also, I don't think that an executive officer was expected to show any great literary or artistic or intellectual qualities. They expected people to be commonsensical, to be reliable chaps who could face a riotous mob or deal with a flood situation and generally make their presence felt in the district.

When fledgeling officers returned to India, fresh from their probationary year, they underwent a thorough vetting by no less a person than the Governor of the province to which they had been posted. Dayal describes what this involved.

I found myself within a few months of arrival from England invited to Government House, which was a very impressive kind of invitation. Three or four other young ICS officers and a couple of police officers had also been similarly asked. The Governor at the time was Sir Malcolm Hailey, who looked like a Roman proconsul, a very able man and a formidable presence. Well, we young people were sort of rotated around the dining-table, and he kept asking in a very casual way what obviously were very searching questions about one's background and one's aptitudes and preferences and so on. After breakfast, he'd say: 'Well, what about taking a walk round the park?' And he'd stride along and we'd go along with him, and he'd keep asking questions about the various trees or birds or flowers. Fortunately, I was interested in gardening, so I could rattle off the names of the flowers. I couldn't do so well with the trees. And he'd ask if we could have a game of tennis in the afternoon. Well, he wasn't a bad player, and one didn't exactly distinguish oneself, but one didn't disgrace oneself either. At the end of the stay, which lasted about a week or ten days, he'd note down in meticulous detail, in a big, black book that he kept, his impressions of each young officer. That was referred to whenever any situation arose. And if you had a good rating from the Governor, well, you could feel fairly secure. Of course, one didn't know what impression one had created.'

Far more than any academic training, the ICS emphasised practical experience in the field. It was customary for new officers to spend their first year or two as assistants to senior British officers, and often to live with them as paying guests during this period. It was a terrifying prospect for young Indian recruits; but many found their British mentors far less stiff and remote than they had expected. Nirmal Mukherji, one of the last batch of ICS recruits before independence and the last of his group to retire, describes his apprenticeship under an outstanding district officer in Firozpur in the Punjab.

When I arrived, I was told, 'He's terrible,' by all my Indian contacts. I was warned: 'You be careful of this man. He's a terrible imperialist in his attitudes.' So naturally I was a little nervous. But I must say that I didn't find any such thing at all. I found him very human. And the very first thing he said to me when I went and called on him was: 'Have you a horse?' I said: 'No, I have only come with a suitcase.' So he said: 'I'm going out on tour tomorrow morning. Can you please join me, and I'll arrange a horse for you?' We went out and toured for the next ten or fifteen days, and it was his way of getting to know me and of putting me wise about how things were done. . . . His *dak* [post] used to come every day; files from the headquarters used to come and go back by courier. And I was made to sit by his side and see all the incoming mail and the outgoing, the orders he had passed or whatever he had written on it, to learn how things were done. In the evenings, we would go out for long walks. And he tried to find out about my family and background and so on. So I thought I'd do the same about *his* family and background. The only time there was a slight embarrassment was when I told him that my parents had been to England a few times and had often remarked at home that the Englishman west of Suez was quite different to the Englishman east of Suez. I asked him to comment on that, and he was a little embarrassed.

The day-to-day work of the colonial district officer was relatively simple and straightforward compared with the complexity of present-day administration. In an age when government played a minimal role in economic development and the provision of social services, there was little need for specialist or technical knowledge. And, until the final decade of the Raj, there were no elected politicians who had to be humoured or obeyed. Nari Rustamji, for instance, found the life of a young officer in charge of his first district rather like 'playing kings and queens'.

I suppose I was 25 or 26 at that time. In those days, there was no telephone where I was, so I couldn't even be ordered to do this or that. I was completely on my own. The post took quite a long time, so even if instructions were sent by government, if they arrived at all, they came late. So you really felt like you were king of your district, wherever you were.

The absence of political control also made for a particularly strong sense of professional independence and camaraderie, as Rajeshwar Dayal explains.

It was a paternalistic and highly centralised system of government. There were no assemblies to whom the administration was answerable, no elected representatives. We young people were put in charge of districts and ruled a million people at the age of thirty or less with no questions asked, accountable to nobody except our seniors in the service, and the service ran the whole administration from the Governor downwards. We were all members of the same service, so there was a sort of fellow-feeling, a service-bond, among us.

Much of a district officer's life was spent travelling round his kingdom, mediating in local disputes and generally 'flying the flag'. At a time when *pukkah* or tarred roads were few and far between, most of this touring was done on horseback, and officers received a generous monthly allowance to maintain a horse and a *syce* or groom. Touring on horseback meant a slow and stately progress through the villages, and many officers, British and Indian, used the opportunity to learn about local conditions and customs. There were others who simply went in search of the best hunting or fishing. But some of the best local studies of people, flora and fauna remain those written by ICS officers.

The ICS took over functions which had been performed for centuries past by the officials of the Mughal empire. What was new was the professionalism and integrity they brought to an administration which, by the time the British arrived, had declined into open nepotism and bribery. A. D. Gorwalla, the oldest surviving Indian member of the service, describes the new administrative ideal.

> You took it for granted that men in high official positions would be honest, that they would regard the people who worked with them as colleagues and not as subordinates. They understood that every person under authority stands on a ladder of subordination, begin- ning with the Viceroy himself right down to the last rung of the ladder who was the *chaprassi* or the peon. They were all under authority. None of them was the master of anybody else, none of them was a boss. They were all people who had their functions and worked within them, each knowing he was a part of the whole thing.

Unlike the early soldiers of fortune who served the East India Company, with their greedy acceptance of the Indian custom of *dastur* or official gifts, the ICS set a remarkably high standard of moral probity. 'The whole administration,' says Rajeshwar Dayal, 'took its tone from the head of the district; and it was reasonably efficient and there was very little corrup- tion. At the very lowest levels of the police force, there was of course the old system of *dastur*, where a certain amount was paid for various services. But above that level, administration was, I think, impeccable.'

According to Dayal, this reputation for personal integrity gave ICS officers a unique moral authority over the villagers in their districts.

> If they saw the Collector himself coming along on horseback and settling a dispute on the spot, they thought that was wonderful. And what was more, they accepted one's judgement. After all, if a case arose, it could be decided one way or the other. But whichever way it was decided, they never questioned the bona fides of the official taking the decision. They didn't say: 'Look, this man has been bribed or he's been unfair.' They'd say: 'Well, he didn't understand my case, and it's my bad luck I lost the case.'

This implicit trust was the basis of the *Maa-Baap Sarkar* (literally 'Mother-Father Government'), on which the paternalistic Raj prided itself. Of course, as with all legends, there was an element of exaggeration in the glorification of the 'Heavenborn'. Ashok Jaitley of the Indian Administrative Service or IAS, which succeeded the ICS after independence, argues that all was not as impeccable as it appeared.

> In the old days, you used to have this system in the ICS where, on *Diwali*[1] and Christmas, the local feudal Nawabs and landlords would send hampers loaded with Scotch whisky and wine and the best of foods and imported cheeses and God knows what else; and that was enough to see you through the year, so you didn't have much expense. During the Second World War, when the whole situation was very difficult in terms of supplies, there were a number of cases of senior civil servants who made their pile in dealing with licences and quotas. There is a story of a District Magistrate in Kanpur, where I was born and where my father used to live. My father told me many years later that [this man] made several lakhs[2] of rupees dispensing petrol during the War; and he was an ICS officer and an Englishman.

Even where there were no pecuniary incentives involved, the ICS did have its own political and social biases. Much has been said of the sympathy of individual British officers for the underdog. But as a rule, the preoccupation of government with enforcing law and order generally favoured the social *status quo* and with it the power of the landed gentry. More radical officers soon found themselves brought into line, as Nari Rustamji reminds us.

> Like many young officers, I came to India with tremendous enthusiasm; and I thought I was going to be a real 'do-gooder'. When I went to my first posting as Assistant Commissioner in Sylhet [Assam], I felt very indignant about the gap between the rich and the poor, and in whatever way I could I wanted to be helpful. I remember some sweepers from the Municipality had come to me and told me that they were being oppressed by the municipal officers and couldn't I help them. In my enthusiasm, I immediately said, 'Yes, of course, I'll hold an inquiry tomorrow.' About twenty sweepers came along to my bungalow, and I heard them all, took evidence from them all, only to be told the very next day that these were all Communists and that I should watch my step. If I wanted to hold an inquiry, I should do it under instructions of the Deputy Commissioner, and I couldn't just go along and hold an inquiry as I liked.

With exceptions like Rustamji, Indian members of the ICS were no more egalitarian than their British colleagues. Coming predominantly from urban, middle-class backgrounds, they were if anything less sympathetic to radical peasant or labour demands. But there was one major political issue which divided the British and Indian halves of the service, and that was the question of Indian nationalism.

1 The Hindu New Year.
2 A *lakh*, an Indian denomination, is 100,000. 100 lakhs make a *crore*, i.e. 10 million.

This was hardly surprising, since the opening up of the ICS to Indians was itself the product of sustained political pressure by the Indian National Congress, the country's main nationalist forum. The peak period of Indian recruitment into the service, from the 1920s to the early 1940s, coincided with the most militant phase of nationalist agitation. Indians in the ICS could not fail to be affected by the prevailing political climate, especially since they came from the same class, and often the same families, as the leadership of Congress. In the present Indian context, it is obviously fashionable for former ICS officers to exaggerate their past nationalism. But even if few acted on their nationalist convictions, the difference between their outlook and that of their British colleagues is widely attested.

In most cases, it took the form of an 'internal reserve' among the Indian half of the service, and occasionally of good-natured banter with British colleagues. Dharam Vir, for instance, describes how his wife, a Congress supporter who had been to gaol for her political activities in the movement, was openly anti-British during the Second World War.

> When the British were losing and France had fallen and the Japanese were coming from the other side, in the club one of the English officers asked: 'Mrs Vir, what do you think? If the Japanese come here, what will you do?' She said: 'What can we do? You have not left us fit to fight. But my husband has a number of garlands. We'll greet them with garlands!' So this man asked me: 'Did you hear her?' I said: 'Yes, I did. I think she's right. She might have been more diplomatic, though.'

British tolerance, however, had its limits. If you were an ambitious young officer, anxious to get on in the service, it was certainly not politic to air your nationalism. According to Dharam Vir, politically suspect officers could not expect to be given charge of a politically sensitive district or to get a secretariat post with access to confidential information. No one was sacked for their political beliefs; but some who acted on their convictions found their careers grinding to a halt. Renuka Ray, the daughter and wife of Indian ICS officers, describes how her father's promotion prospects were blighted by his spontaneous reaction to an incident of police brutality. He was one of the earliest batch of Indian ICS recruits and served as the district officer at Khulna (Bengal) shortly before the First World War. 'When he went to this district,' says his daughter, 'he was quite popular, because he was good at games, he could play polo and he was a good rider.' One day, he got a call to say that there was trouble at a local police station. He rushed there to find that a group of students and lawyers had been handcuffed and beaten up by the police for shouting the nationalist slogan 'Vande Mataram' (I bow to thee, my Motherland) in the street. He immediately ordered the handcuffs to be removed and made the police apologise. Although the British Superintendant of Police had to submit to the superior authority of an Indian District Magistrate, he complained to Divisional Headquarters, whence the matter was referred to the top authorities in Calcutta.

After prolonged investigations, involving a visit by no less a person than the Lieutenant-Governor, Mrs Ray's father was eventually cleared of misconduct. 'But that did not convince these people,' she says, 'and they decided that he did not deserve any promotions. He was a District Magistrate then, and he remained a District Magistrate till he retired.'

Most Indian officers, especially during the political turmoil of the 1930s and 1940s, found more tactful ways of reconciling their orders with their political consciences, as Rajeshwar Dayal explains.

> The best thing was to remain absolutely discreet and quiet and not to show one's sympathies one way or the other. The British were somewhat sensitive also to the susceptibilities and sensibilities of the Indian officers by not forcing them into impossible situations, except, of course, during the Quit India movement of 1943 when one found oneself willy-nilly face to face with this type of situation. Many of us did feel very strongly that we had divided loyalties. I didn't take some of the measures which I was expected to, such as the collective fines and wholesale arrests. And my explanation was asked as to why I hadn't taken certain measures which had been recommended. My reply was that my district was comparatively quiet, and if I had taken action of that type it might have been counter-productive, it might have created an uproar, an upheaval, so I thought it was better to let sleeping dogs lie. That explanation was more or less accepted, but I found myself transferred to the Secretariat, which I didn't regret at all since it saved me from any further embarrassing situations.

Political divisions within the ICS were reinforced by the widespread feeling among Indian members that they were not really socially acceptable to the British half. This lack of social acceptance consigned Indian officers to a sort of no-man's land. The more anglicised you were, the better your promotion prospects; and 'going native' in your culture and habits was definitely frowned upon, even if you were Indian. 'We found ourselves in a very invidious position,' says Dayal. 'One was not expected to be hob-nobbing with the notables of the town by joining their club, except for going to play a game of bridge, because in bridge you don't have to make any conversation or establish any personal rapport with anybody. But at the same time, we were not admitted, at least in the United Provinces, to the service club as full members. We could only became honorary members; and we Indian officers thought it was *infra dig* to accept that sort of situation.'

The result was that the British and Indian halves of the administration tended to lead parallel but separate lives within their own narrow social circles. This was particularly noticeable during Civil Service Week, when ICS officers from the districts thronged the provincial capital to attend a series of dances and dinners, including a ball at Government House. 'At the most, we received invitations to tea and tennis from the British seniors,' Dayal recalls. 'We were never invited to stay with them. But we were invited to stay with the Indian ministers and senior officials. The

Indians seemed to have parallel functions going on, so it was a rather peculiar situation.'

At work, says Dayal, relations between British and Indian officers were polite and amicable, but rarely any warmer.

> Unfortunately, one made very few friends with the British officers. I had British subordinates and seniors. In the Secretariat, we called each other by our first names, and at the most we'd invite each other to a cocktail, but never to dinner. . . . We somehow learned to keep our distance. For instance, at a Government House ball, one would not ask an English lady to dance. And hardly any British officers would ask any Indian lady to the floor. And all the Indians, including the ministers and very senior officials, would be sitting on one side, and the British would be on the other side. So there was this sort of social chasm.

British exclusiveness ensured that the very Indians who owed the most to the Raj, and on whom colonial rule most depended, remained ambivalent in their loyalty to it. They were the chosen few; and the British gave them vast power and privilege over their own countrymen. But however hard they tried, they could not escape the fact that they would always be treated as second-best in a colonial service.

Indian officers who trained under the British did not resent learning from colonial mentors. But most of them saw this as no more than a necessary apprenticeship for the day, not so far away, when the British would have to leave. 'We had it in the back of our minds,' says Nirmal Mukherji, 'that independence was around the corner, and that when independence came it would require civil servants of some kind.' Narottam Sahgal, one of the Indians most loyal to the ICS, confirms that, by the 1930s, the end of the Raj seemed inevitable.

> Obviously, as an Indian one was extremely wedded to the idea of an independent country. There was absolutely no reason why we should continue to be just part of an empire. By the time I was in the service, it was pretty clear that the British days were numbered in this country. It was just a question of whether they'd leave with good grace or there'd be trouble.

SERVING THE SAHIBS
RULING BY LAW

Being an independent profession, we had more chance to deviate
than the chap who had to depend for his money on government.
We didn't have to depend on government for anything at all. That's
why people like Gandhiji, Pandit Jawaharlal Nehru and his father,
Motilal Nehru, most of the top leaders before independence, were
from the Bar; and that's why they could devote such a tremendous
amount of time to politics. They were the only intelligentsia who
were absolutely independent of any governmental influence.

Govind Swaminathan (former Advocate-General, Madras)

Indian law and justice were not British inventions. The Hindu and Muslim rulers whom the British succeeded had had their own judicial administration, based largely on religious custom. As with the rest of the administration, colonial legal reformers were pragmatic enough to retain as much as possible of the old order, especially in the sphere of personal and civil law. Nevertheless, more by necessity than design, colonial law and its instruments evolved progressively on the British model.

Those were times when the enforcement of law and order was regarded as the main duty of government; and this was particularly true for a colonial government, which was there, as was often said, 'to rule, not serve'. The British preoccupation with India's judicial administration had less to do with any ideological commitment to exporting British justice than with the practical need for a clearly defined body of law, which could be efficiently administered across the sub-continent.

During the first phase of British rule, from the mid-eighteenth to the mid-nineteenth century, the Indian legal scene remained a bewildering medley of at least three competing types of jurisdiction, with 'country' or 'native' courts in the districts administering traditional justice, the East India Company's courts determining revenue and civil matters, and Crown courts meting out British justice to British subjects. It was not till the 1860s that this free-for-all was rationalised into the single, uniform system which the Raj later bequeathed to independent India. Its main elements were a codified civil and criminal law for the whole of British India, administered by provincial high courts modelled on the British Crown Court, with jurisdiction over subordinate sessions and district courts and a right of appeal to the Privy Council in London.

The codification of the law and the right of the judiciary to enforce it against government were the most revolutionary features of these reforms in a society where law had been largely customary, and therefore subject to arbitrary application by the princes who administered it and the religious authorities who interpreted it. The Raj may have been as despotic as its predecessors; but even its harshest critics agree that it was not, in the main, arbitrary. As S. K. Acharyya, former left-wing Advocate-General of West Bengal, put it, even when the British wanted to oppress people, they first made a law giving themselves the right to do it.

Obviously, the rule of law could not be democratic, so long as an unelected and foreign government made the laws. But it did at least mean that the principle of government itself being subject to the law was well established. The Raj could and did enact repressive measures censoring the press, banning political activity and providing for preventive detention. But the High Courts had the right to review abuses of executive power and to issue writs of *Habeas Corpus*, a right they did use occasionally to free political prisoners and defend civil liberties.

Equally important, at least in theory, was the principle of equality before the law. British Indian courts recognised no distinction of caste or religion among Indians. The only exceptions were the British themselves, who, until 1883, could not be tried by Indian judges. Until the end of the Raj, British defendants could claim the privilege of being tried by a half-European jury. But according to a leading Indian lawyer like Govind Swaminathan, the last Crown Prosecutor of Madras, this privilege was not as discriminatory as it appeared, because European juries usually felt obliged to set an example by being harsher with their own kind than Indian jurors would have been.

The converse of this was also true. A former barrister in Bombay remembers a murder trial in the 1930s in which he got the defendant acquitted, despite overwhelming evidence against him, by the expedient of getting an all-European jury, which, as anticipated, proved reluctant to send an Indian to the gallows.

A more important limitation on equality before the law was the expense of litigation in a country where the gap between rich and poor was far wider than in Britain. In India, economic disparities were compounded by the fact that the court language was English, and therefore unknown to the vast majority of litigants and witnesses. But the intervention of dedicated judges seems to have ensured that the scales were not as heavily weighted as they might have been in favour of the affluent, English-speaking élite. H. M. Seervai, a veteran of the Bombay Bar, says he can remember several occasions when a British judge, finding someone's knowledge of English or the law inadequate, would come to the rescue and present the arguments himself.

The language barrier was also bridged by the services of experienced interpreters. Govind Swaminathan describes how their intervention, far from being tiresome, added drama to the proceedings.

> Questions had to be asked in English, the answer had to come in English. The witness had not a clue about English, so you had a top-class interpreter. My question would be interpreted beautifully to the witness. The witness would answer, and that would be interpreted beautifully for the aid of the jury and the judge. And some interpreters were really born actors, when you'd come to a

key point or key question for the defence, and the interpreter would get into the spirit of the thing and ask it in the same tone that counsel had asked it.

As H. M. Seervai reminds us, there were also times when interpreters got confused, causing a certain amount of unintended mirth.

Occasionally, humorous answers were given by literal translation. For example, one of the judges asked the interpreter to tell the witness not to tell unnecessary lies. And the interpreter said: 'Tell lies only when it is necessary.'

Many Indians believe that truth was the first casualty in the adversarial system of justice which British rules of evidence introduced, with the litigants like rivals in a boxing-ring and the judge as referee. They argue that a more inquisitorial system, with an active, investigating magistrate, might have been better suited to Indian conditions. British justice, with its rigid and impersonal procedures, was certainly alien to a people accustomed to the informal and more intimate disputations of traditional *panchayats* (village tribunals) or to the role of humble supplicants at princely *durbars*. British Indian courts made few concessions to the Indian ethos. With the exception of wigs, which were judged impractical in the Indian climate, their ritual and procedure, as Govind Swaminathan describes them, were closely patterned on the Old Bailey.

The whole panoply was gone through on the day the sessions opened. The Sheriff marched first with his mace, then the judge in his red robes. They came into court, and a clerk of the court shouted: 'Oyez, Oyez, Oyez!' ... that kind of nonsense. The jury were empanelled; and at the beginning the jury was mostly British, but gradually we found more Indians on the jury.

The law itself was a pragmatic compromise between the secular principles of British justice and the Indian religious law that continued to rule marriage, inheritance and many other civil matters. The fusion of two such opposite legal philosophies could sometimes produce situations which bordered on the ridiculous. Khushwant Singh, a Sikh who practised in Lahore as a young barrister in the 1940s, still laughs with glee over the discomfiture of a British judge presented with a particularly embarrassing piece of evidence.

Justice Falshaw was then a Sessions judge trying the case of a Muslim who claimed to have married a very rich Sikh widow and sired several children through her. His case was that she'd been converted to Islam; and as a symbol or gesture of her conversion, she had cut off her hair, which was forbidden by the Sikh faith. His lawyer produced the evidence in an envelope and placed it before Justice Falshaw and said: 'Here is conclusive evidence of this woman having abandoned the Sikh faith.' And Falshaw asked him: 'What exactly is it?' He said: 'Sir, this is her pubic hair, which she shaved.' Falshaw was absolutely scandalised, and he screamed: 'Take it off my table at once!'

The clash of cultures in the courtrooms of the Raj was less glaring than it might have been because it was mediated by a large and growing legal profession, which was increasingly at home in both cultures. The judges of the higher courts remained mostly British until independence, recruited from the judicial branch of the ICS and, to a lesser extent, from the Bar. But as Govind Swaminathan points out, they were far from ignorant of Indian customs or conditions.

> They knew what witnesses were meaning when they said: 'How long did it take you to go from here to there?' – 'Well, it took me the time it would take me to eat a *paan* [betel leaf].' They knew what that meant. And they also knew that most eye-witnesses were eye-witnesses because they went to answer a call of nature and they happened to be outside. They knew the exact position of streetlights and how much light our Indian street-lights give off for the question of identification. The ICS people were marvellous because they'd been in the districts. They'd come up from being a magistrate, and they'd learnt everything in the districts . . . they could speak the language. I can't remember an occasion when you had to explain anything to them in great detail. And even the Privy Council in England could sit down and listen to a case, argued probably by English lawyers, on what direction the temple-marks on an elephant's forehead should go, after examining all the customs.

Grassroots experience in the districts was certainly a powerful judicial asset, even if it produced some unorthodox methods of disposing of litigation. Narottam Sahgal, an Indian member of the ICS, tells the story of how a British magistrate made time for his hunting by ridding himself of tiresome litigants.

> His disposal in criminal cases was remarkable. When the case came up, he'd first ask them very solemnly whether they'd thought of compromising the matter. Of course, at that stage they'd say they were going to proceed with the case. And he'd say: 'All right. I'm very busy right now, so please go and sit outside, and I'll send for you later.' Now, in summer it gets very, very hot, and the officer had given instructions that they were to be given no water or any other facilities and that they were just to sit there and discuss the matter with each other and try and effect a compromise. After he'd sent for them three or four times and they'd said no, they hadn't compromised, at about five in the evening he'd send for them again. And if they still hadn't compromised, the next day the same thing would happen. And then they realised that it was better to compromise than sit in the heat all day long; and they'd come and say: 'Yes, we've compromised.'

The Indian Bar was almost wholly a product of the colonial impact. Before that, legal representation had required no professional qualifications or training beyond religious learning. From the middle of the nineteenth century, this informality gave way to an organised and secular legal profession, based on law faculties and degrees at the new British Indian universities. Initially, the Bar was dominated by Europeans. But as its numbers expanded, so did the process of Indianisation. By the turn of the century, a majority of High Court advocates were Indians; and in the next two decades, British lawyers rapidly became extinct.

The fact that the judicial benches remained predominantly European, while the legal profession was almost entirely Indian, made these two branches of the legal system far more separate than in Britain. The splendid isolation of the judiciary, who stood aloof from the usual social and personal influences, was probably an important factor in the impartiality for which British judges in India were renowned. Khushwant Singh remembers how difficult it was for an Indian barrister to establish any social contact with British judges.

> You met them in court, and that was it. The very first time I made a breakthrough was when my wife's cousin got the Victoria Cross. He was the first Indian to win it, and I thought this was a good opportunity for me to exploit. So I threw a cocktail party and invited all the English judges to meet the first Indian winner of the Victoria Cross, and they all came. And then suddenly everything changed. Thereafter, if I invited them home they came, and I was always treated with much greater courtesy, because that confirmed in their minds that I belonged to a family who were willing to fight on the side of the British with enough enthusiasm.

At a time when commerce was still dominated by British firms, and Indian industry was in its infancy, the law was virtually the only independent profession open to Indians outside the government services; and it soon became the most popular career for middle-class Indians who avoided or were rejected by the services. Being a lawyer had certain advantages over the civil service, because it offered a lucrative income and high social status along with independence from government. It was not coincidental that the Bar became a training for nationalist politics, or that most of the nationalist leaders, including Mahatma Gandhi and the Nehrus, started their careers as lawyers. From practising law to wanting to make it, was not, after all, such a big step.

SERVING THE SAHIBS
SOLDIERS OF EMPIRE

*The British officer introduced the concept of officerhood. He made
the Indian Army. The armies of the Mughals and the Indian princes
tended to be a whole mass army. So when the top fell, or was seen
to be shot down from his elephant, or the rumour went round that
the leader was dead, everyone tended to run. It was panic. Now, the
East India Company's best export to India was these young men
from middle-class Britain, with their background of education and
certain values, which included sticking with their men in adversity,
not running in battle, as they proved in many generations of
soldiering in Europe. They formed the firming in part
of the Indian other ranks, as the regular officer in regiments
which we never had before.*

'Monty' Palit (General, Indian Army – retired)

*The British Indian army was, after all, a mercenary army. The
officers and* jawans *were serving in it in order to get a good salary
and have a good life.*

Tony Bhagat (Brigadier, Indian Army – retired.
Also served as an officer in the rebel Indian National Army)

Britain's empire-builders were proud of the fact that they had won India
by the sword; and the military might of the Raj remained until the end
the ultimate sanction of imperial power. What is mentioned less often is
that it was Indian troops who enabled a British trading company to
conquer and hold a vast sub-continent so distant from British shores.
And later, it was the sepoys of the East India Company's Bengal Army
who led the first and most serious revolt against British rule in 1857.

The modern, professional army which the British bequeathed to
independent India and Pakistan dates back to the major reorganisation
which took place after the Mutiny of 1857. The British were quick to
recognise that a major cause of the Mutiny had been the religious
grievances of Brahmin and other upper-caste troops in the Bengal Army,
recruited from India's Hindu heartland. The changes that followed were
designed to ensure that British Indian troops would never again have a
rebellious nucleus capable of coordinating a national uprising. The result
was a new regimental structure clearly based on the principle of divide
and rule, as 'Monty' Palit, a retired Indian general, explains.

You only have to read the reports and deliberations of a number of
commissions set up by Her Majesty's Government in England and
by the Viceroy in India, all of which were asked, since a native army
(as they called it) was necessary, how to organise this army so that

23

the rebellion of 1857, which they called the Mutiny, would never take place again. By and large, the consensus was that the only way to do it was to have natives fight natives, Sikhs shoot Hindus, Hindus shoot on Muslims, and the Gurkhas shoot all Indians. They would keep regiments, or sub-units like companies, of particular cadres, so that Indians would never get a sense of cohesion as a nation.

The new Indian army was recruited predominantly from areas which had remained loyal to the British during the Mutiny – Sikhs, Muslims and Rajputs in the north-west and Gurkhas from Nepal in the north-east. These were warrior-castes, traditionally aloof from politics; and they were designated the 'martial races' of the empire. They were divided up into tribal regiments, which were themselves usually sub-divided into separate, ethnic units at company level. The Punjab Regiment, for instance, was made up of Sikhs, Punjabi Muslims and Hindu Dogras, each with their separate units. It was a system calculated to build strong regimental loyalties which would override any sense of nationalism or political disaffection. And it kept command firmly in the hands of the ruling race. While the lower ranks and the non-commissioned officers were entirely Indian, the officer corps was entirely British.

The Raj maintained a peacetime standing army of about 200,000 troops, roughly a third of whom were British and served in separate British army regiments stationed in India. British and Indian regiments were kept completely apart, with little mixing between their British officers and none at all between the other ranks.

It was against this background that demands began to grow, especially after the First World War, for Indianisation of the officer corps of the Indian Army. This was seen partly as a just reward for the sacrifices made by Indian troops in the war, but also as a logical corollary to the process of political reform which was gradually opening up senior posts to Western-educated, middle-class Indians.

It was a process far more fiercely resisted in the army than in the civilian services. The army was, after all, the bastion of European racial supremacy, and its officers were even less accustomed to mixing with Indian social equals than their ICS counterparts. Though the Raj made some concessions to Indianisation, the entry of Indian officers remained a mere trickle, confined to a handful who managed to get to Sandhurst and qualify for the King's Commission. It was not until the late 1930s that provision was made for Indian commissions, with an Indian Military Academy (IMA), modelled on Sandhurst, set up for this purpose.

One of the first batch of officer cadets trained at the IMA, Brigadier Tony Bhagat, remembers that the struggle did not end there. The new Indian commissioned officers found themselves on a substantially lower pay-scale compared with British colleagues and encountered humiliating attempts to hive them off into separate mess facilities.

Another product of the IMA, General J. S. Aurora, later the hero of India's military victory over Pakistan in the 1971 Bangladesh War, describes the initial British reaction to Indianisation.

I think they resented Indianisation; and one did come across a certain number of officers who were apt to run down or be unduly supercilious about the Indians. When it came to giving choice appointments and commands, the Indian officers did not get them. In fact, at one time it was proposed that the Indian commissioned officers should have a separate mess. But I think it was soon realised that that was going to make it extremely difficult for the Indian commissioned officers to get the respect that they must have if they were going to command troops. So, mercifully, this was not put into practice.

Ironically, young Indian officers often found that they were more warmly received by the British army regiments where they had to spend a year as part of their training. General Aurora, for instance, spent six months with the Argyll and Sutherland Highlanders and another six months with the King's Own Scottish Borderers. 'We found that the young officers were quite friendly really,' he recalls, 'and they made you feel reasonably welcome. The British Army was not being affected by Indianisation; so their attitude was that they took you at your face value. If you were somebody who fitted in, they liked you. If you were aloof or wanted to be on your own, they left you alone.'

Another retired general, 'Monty' Palit, was one of the few Indians to get a King's commission at Sandhurst. He came from a family with strong martial traditions, seven generations having served in the Mughal cavalry before colonial rule cut Indians off from officer rank. He points out that Indianisation, in its early stages, did little to redress the balance.

They granted it grudgingly – a very small number every year. But they didn't want the Indians to mix with; so they earmarked certain battalions in each regiment and put all the Indians there – made ghettos in the regiments and put us all there. From 1925 this happened till 1939, when the war broke out. We lived amongst ourselves in our little battalions, and they lived in their regiments and battalions with no Indian officers. There was no mixing of them at all ... When I joined my regiment, the Baluch, the Commanding Officer and three seniors, company commanders, were British. I never went to their homes. Nobody ever asked me for a drink or tea or anything. We lived amongst ourselves. We had our own social life – that was in Peshawar.[1] We joined the club, of course; but we only went there for games. I never once saw an Indian officer ever share a table with a British officer or his wife. There were some who sought the company of the British – we called them toadies.

With the outbreak of the Second World War, this situation changed quite dramatically, as European racial exclusiveness had to take second place to the demands of active service. Indians found themselves welcome

[1] Capital of the North-West Frontier Province, now in Pakistan.

in most regiments, and a few were even given command of British subordinates. But there were still reminders that they were there on British terms. Mess life followed its old Anglo-Indian rituals, and Indian officers had to conform. There was a strong emphasis on being anglicised. Indian music was frowned upon; eating with your hands was strictly out; and worst of all, Indian food was rarely served. Even in wartime, says General Aurora, mess menus could provoke major rows.

The Indian meals were limited to two lunches a week, and the rest of the time the food had to be British, whereas for most of us the British food did not suit our palate. Therefore we had to find ways and means of supplementing it and even having food from the *jawan*[1] messes. . . . We were out in Singapore, and I was made the food member. So I said we'll change one thing – whereas we'll have the meat as it is done, instead of giving boiled vegetables we'll have them light-fried. I gave that instruction to the cook. He didn't carry it out; so I asked him why he had not carried out my orders, and he said it was too much work for him. I said: 'No, you have an assistant, and you will damn well carry them out and fry these things!' Next day I was called up by the President of the Mess: 'I believe you have threatened the cook?' I said: 'Yes, I have. He did not carry out my orders, because I wanted him to fry the vegetables as opposed to serving them boiled.' He said: 'But you have your two Indian meals a week in any case.' So I said: 'Listen, as the messing member my job is to give food to people that they would like to eat. And if this chap does not carry out my orders, I think I've got my rights.' All that happened was that I was changed as a messing member and somebody else was put in my place. That did start a little vendetta between that senior officer and myself.

The arrogance of British officers accustomed to dealing only with Indian lower ranks could be particularly galling to Indians who came from an upper-class background. One of them, Rashid Ali Baig, who went from a British public school to Sandhurst, later became independent India's first Chief of Protocol. His widow explains why he resigned his army commission under the Raj.

He was absolutely shocked when he came out to India and found that the Englishman in India was a totally different animal – it wasn't the same person. In the end, he resigned from the army, because he was very proud. He came from a Hyderabad[2] family that had their own pride; and he wasn't going to stand it from people who were definitely not the sort of person that you'd invite to dinner.

Even more important than such social tensions between Indian and British officers was the discord between them over the nationalist movement. While most Indian officers served their regiments

[1] Private soldier.
[2] Then India's largest princely state, ruled by the Muslim Nizam dynasty.

loyally throughout the Second World War, many of them were nevertheless intensely nationalistic. A few actually defected to the Indian National Army or INA, which fought on the Japanese side, and many more felt a sneaking admiration for the INA and a growing resentment about the contempt with which British seniors regarded Indian nationalism. Although politics were officially out of bounds in the mess, the subject did crop up from time to time, as General Aurora reports.

Most of us, when we discussed anything among ourselves, were pro-nationalist. Anything that Jawaharlal Nehru said or did or any programme that Mahatma Gandhi laid down, we were totally in sympathy with that. There were cases when we had arguments in the mess. In 1946 or early '47, I was sitting in the mess at the breakfast table when there was a discussion going on about how fast India should get independence. The general tone was that they must learn to walk before they want to run. I was the only Indian officer in that group at the time. So the commandant turned round to me and said: 'What do you think about it?' I said: 'Look here, sir, you have been ruling India for such a long time, you can say from 1857. And according to you we haven't learnt to walk yet. At this stage, I don't think we ever will learn. So why the hell are you bothered about us? You leave us to our own designs.' There was a stunned silence. I came home and told my wife that I may be asked to pack my bags. But that gentleman a few days later invited my wife and myself to have lunch with him, and we became rather friendly. So this was a case in which my outspokenness did not go against me. But there have been cases, I do know, where people were watched very carefully and their future would be affected.

Most Indian officers, says General Palit, preferred to be discreet about their politics.

In our Indianised battalion, I found several officers who had studied the political movement and were very Congress-minded, and I was enthused by all this. But we had to be careful not to let the British know that this kind of activity or talk was going on. It was still in the days when one's career could be cut off just because you happened to express admiration for Gandhi or Nehru.

The war years did help to end the isolation of Indians, with the arrival of large numbers of young British officers who did not share the old Anglo-Indian prejudices. When political arguments arose, they often sided with the Indians against the British die-hards, as Palit discovered when he took on a particularly bigoted colonel of the old school.

On every occasion, he would try and expound his very limited intellectual capacity for Indian politics and always look at me. By that time there were lots of British officers who would have supported me, so I got a little more courage and I did answer him back once or twice. For instance, once he said: 'I know exactly what I'm going to do in India when the war ends. There's going to be Gandhi and Nehru and Jinnah, and they're going to fight each other. And we shall take our loot and go home. Isn't that clever, Palit?' I said: 'Very clever, because you've been doing it for two hundred years.' His face fell and he went red, but as people laughed there was no come-back.

The last bastions of British supremacy in the Indian Army were the Gurkha regiments, which had been set up by special arrangement with the Maharaja of Nepal after he helped suppress the Mutiny of 1857. No Indian had ever been allowed to command Gurkha troops; and when the inevitable transfer came, shortly before independence, it encountered intense British hostility. General Palit describes his experience as a young colonel taking over a Gurkha regiment soon after the end of the war.

It was like going to a British regiment and suddenly the British officers being told to get out because the Indians were coming. My predecessor was a very well-decorated soldier of great renown, but he wouldn't play fair with me. I asked him what the feeling was among the men and the officers, and he said: 'Everything is fine.' But within a few days, I realised that they'd been talking against us to the Gurkhas. They'd been saying: 'Bengali Babus¹ are coming to take over your battalion. They'll never fight with you. They'll let you down in battle. You'd best go home.' It was rather a sad tale because I never realised that the British would play so dirty.

According to Palit, such spite went beyond hostile gossip.

One of the Indian officers came to me and said: 'Sir, the British have taken all the silver away.' I said: 'Let them take anything away. I don't mind – we're taking the regiment over.' But the mess sergeant came to me and said: 'Sahib, I am the man responsible for all this in my books, and it's all been sent away – some to British Army regiments . . . some to private pockets, and all the crockery has been broken up, all the old stocks of wine have been opened and the gardens swamped with them. What am I going to do about all this?' So I wrote to the Indian centre commander who had just taken over from the British, and he wrote to our former colonel, and they got every piece of silver except one back for us.

Such experiences were not unique. Similar panic and hostility marked the Indian takeover of other Gurkha regiments; and there were cases of British officers even transferring regimental funds to British bank accounts for safekeeping.

Until the last years of the Raj, British relations with the Indian lower ranks were remarkably free of the tensions that marred contact between British and Indian officers. With the *jawans* and non-commissioned officers, the British maintained a benevolent paternalism, similar to that of the *Ma-Baap Sarkar* in civilian life. The strong loyalty of the *jawans* to

---

¹ Clerks.

their regiments and their British officers was the product of more than half a century of selective recruitment from particular ethnic groups, often from the same villages and families. But where this traditional recruitment pattern broke down, as it did in the navy, the results could be far more dangerous to the Raj than the armchair nationalism of Indian officers.

The Royal Indian Navy was a relatively new service which expanded almost overnight during the Second World War to counter the Japanese advance in the East. When the war began, its total strength was five 'small tubs', with around 1500 men commanded by half a dozen British officers. By the end of the war, its numbers had grown to more than 45,000. The new recruits came, not merely from the so-called 'martial races', but from all over the country, wherever they could be found. Many of them, especially the communications ratings, were not illiterate peasants, like the army *jawans*, but educated young men from a lower-middle-class background. And since naval ships and shore establishments did not allow for the ethnic separation of military barracks, ratings from different communities were integrated to an extent unprecedented in Indian life, as one of them, B. C. Dutt, explains.

> Once a man joined the navy, he ate the same food, slept in the same place and all lived together, whether he belonged to Kashmir or Kanyakumari.[1] And that was a very big difference, because ratings by and large all came from the villages. And a boy from remote Assam and a boy from a village of Maharashtra beginning to live together can be difficult at the beginning. But they learned to live together; and in six months' time they developed a kind of camaraderie which was altogether different from that which prevailed in the army.

Most of the navy's new officers were volunteers from civilian life, who lacked the professionalism of regular officers and had little rapport with their men. Many ratings, for their part, were teenagers from remote villages and, like B. C. Dutt, had never seen a white man before. Dutt describes how his feelings of awe for British officers quickly turned to dismay when he arrived at a military training camp.

> It was raining hard, month of July. We reached there at about 7 o'clock in the evening. It was all dark, and we were made to fall in there. Lieutenant Gorfit [one of the instructors] started. He said: 'You bastards! You have been brought here so that I can make you tough, because you are going to fight. It's going to be a real fight, and I'm going to see that you are made tough even if it takes me a hundred years. . . . Don't forget that you have sold your bloody souls for sixty rupees a month, and now the souls are in my hands, and I'll see that they are turned into fighting people. You bastards, dismissed! Go to your barracks!' And what were the barracks?

1 India's southern tip.

There was no light, absolute cowshed. And just about five hundred yards away, you could see lights and beautiful barracks where Britishers were living. . . . My age? Nineteen. Not only my blood boiled, every single one, even the 'Anglo-Indian'[1] boys were aghast.

Not all British instructors were so harsh or insensitive. Dutt also remembers a Lieutenant Yorker, who 'was always trying to make up for his brother officers'. But Yorker had to pay for his popularity among the ratings. He was labelled a 'wog-lover' in the Officers' Mess. British officers boycotted him; he had to eat alone at his own table; and a few months later, he was replaced by an inexperienced, new officer.

The war necessitated some departures from the long-established tradition of keeping Indian and British lower ranks far apart. During combined operations in Burma, Indian naval ratings were thrown into close proximity to white troops from Britain and other Commonwealth countries. And they soon discovered that their separate facilities involved a large measure of racial discrimination. The contrast was particularly obvious in living conditions at the combined operations training-camp on Mahd Island, near Bombay, which B. C. Dutt describes.

British, white soldiers were always kept separately: separate camp, separate hospital, everything separate, and better for anybody to see. White people's place of entertainment, that side we were not allowed to go, so naturally there was no question of meeting them. If there was an English film-show, which many of us who could understand the language wanted to go to, we were not allowed to go near, even if there was space to sit in the tent, shooed off. Their canteen – they had everything they wanted. We had a little cowshed. We could get some biscuits perhaps, and that's about all, nothing else there.

Even in battle, these distinctions were not relaxed. If anything, says Dutt, Indian sailors felt the humiliation and hardship of their inferior status even more keenly during active service.

We were a small group from the Royal Indian Navy attached to the army that invaded Burma. We were the communications ratings, and the invading army were Indians, British and Australians. Wherever we landed, we always, invariably, saw that we were the last to be taken back off the beach. The first chance, after the battle was over and soldiers were to be taken back, white people were taken out first. We might be hanging around there for a day or two. When you've been in battle-dress on the beach, fighting for three or four days; you haven't had hot meals; you haven't had a bath; you've been drinking water from your bottle or no water at all, then your whole body cries out for a hot meal and a bath. But you're hanging out there, with all the facilities for taking the soldiers out first extended to the Britishers, then other white people, and then us.

1 In its later usage, referring to India's 200,000-strong community of mixed British and Indian descent.

The transport system? If we were taken from one place to another, one hundred of us, the same space would be allocated to a maximum of twenty or thirty Britishers. They must have sleeping accommodation; we never dreamt of sleeping accommodation. They tried their best to keep us separate. But if we came into contact, their attitude, their talk, their language, there was no question of hiding it. The greeting was: 'Hi, black bastard!' It was so bad that in my regiment or group, which consisted of practically all the communities of India, including 'Anglo-Indians' who had been very pro-British, every single one of us by the time we came back from the battlefront were all anti-British.

Such anger lay at the root of the Naval Mutiny which erupted in 1946; and by then, similar rumblings of discontent in some army and airforce units led the authorities to fear that the trouble might spread through the armed forces generally. It is now generally acknowledged that post-war disaffection in the armed forces, with its echoes of 1857, was the last straw which broke the Raj and hastened the imperial retreat. Whether in the growing friction between British and Indian officers, or in the crumbling loyalty of the lower ranks, it was clear by the end of the Second World War that the system which the Raj had devised to guarantee the obedience of its Indian troops had outlived its usefulness and could no longer be relied upon.

BANYAS & BOXWALLAHS

The Indian style of business was highly personalised. Being under family control, the consultation, advice, policy-making was all done within the family. In fact, in many families they had a system of a sort of evening get-together, including wives, where they would discuss the problems of the business and the day. Whereas in British firms there was a professionalism, rather more like government service. And that's why one or two offers I had to join large Indian firms, I didn't take because of this highly personal atmosphere.

Prakash Tandon (former executive, Lever Brothers)

'Boxwallah' was the Anglo-Indian term for the British businessman in India. It originated with the boxes in which traders used to carry their samples when they travelled up-country. The term acquired pejorative overtones, similar to 'travelling saleman', and by association it was applied to the business profession generally. Although the British started out as traders and retained until the end a strong economic stake in India, businessmen ranked lowest in the professional and social hierarchy of the Raj.

The Indian equivalent of the boxwallahs were the *banyas* – the merchant community who ranked below priests and warriors in the Hindu caste system. During the early phase of empire, they were the Indians who had the most contact with the British, as the local brokers, moneylenders and sales agents who serviced the trade of the East India Company and its successors.

In 1833, the East India Company lost its monopoly of the India trade; and there followed a period of free enterprise which lasted into the 1920s. Many of the new British Indian firms which sprang up during this period were established by former Company servants who started out as agents for other British firms. They founded what were known as Managing Agency Houses, a peculiarly Anglo-Indian type of business organisation that lasted until well after independence. In essence, it consisted of a single well-established company entrusted with the management of a large number of other firms, often owned by different shareholders and dealing in different types of products. Its great advantage was that it allowed for coordinated business planning and for the pooling of resources between different sectors of the economy. But it also lent itself to the creation of monopolistic and hereditary business empires, often controlled by a single family concern.

Until the First World War, which provided a major stimulus to Indian business, a handful of British managing agencies had a near-monopoly of India's foreign trade and its infant industries. These industries were confined to the manufacture of the raw materials and semi-agricultural products which the imperial economy required – coal for the imperial railways, and tea, jute and cotton for the British home market. The firms which ran these industries were owned and managed by Europeans; and no Indian could expect employment in them above the level of clerks. But British business did rely extensively on what might now be called an Indian 'comprador' or collaborating business class – a network of indigenous brokers and agents. Many Indian agents made themselves indispensable to British firms; and some rose to be partners and, eventually, even proprietors of the firms they once served.

One example is the Mathuradas Vissanji business house in Bombay, which now owns the old British firm of Shaw Wallace, and manufactures products ranging from flour to electronics. The office of the present head of the House of Vissanji, in a musty Victorian block in Bombay's Wallace Street, has changed very little since the days of the nineteenth-century British founders. According to Pratapsinh Vissanji, his family's association with Shaw Wallace dates back to 1857, the year of the Mutiny, when his grandfather became the carting agent for the firm's cotton trade. Thirty years later, his business acumen had made him so valuable to the firm that the Wallace family took him in as a partner. His word was law in the Bombay office; and his grandson describes what happened when a European employee tried to cross him.

> He was equal to the British partners; so all British subordinates who were working for the firm were also subordinate to him. His opinion always carried much more weight than any of the subordinate staff. There have been instances where, if in his opinion a certain person was not up to standard, he was really packed off. There was an instance where one of the men was packed off in just twenty-four hours. One of the bills that my grandfather had signed, this employee questioned his bill and it was sent back. So my grandfather sent back the bill along with his resignation, which the senior partners of the British firm could not accept. They themselves came and took him up to their office; and there the employee had to apologise to him, and after that he was packed off the very next day.

This partnership became a hereditary arrangement which endured through three generations of the Vissanji and Wallace families. But, as Pratapsinh Vissanji recalls, it was subject to a stringent test of ability, which he himself had to undergo when he joined the business in the 1930s.

> They had one clause in the arrangement: that whoever succeeds must have the approval of the managing director or chairman of the company. Their tests were very, very strict. When I came in, my father and my uncle, who were the approved people, had to withdraw for one year; and I was put independently in charge. I had to predict certain results well in advance, which were analysed

at the end of the year. Fortunately for me, I was 92 per cent right. Then only they accepted me, and my name was included in the agreement. Otherwise that agreement would have come to termination.

Experience of this kind prepared the way for the independent expansion of Indian businesses, as former agents of British firms started going into business on their own account. Before the British, the traditional Indian form of business organisation had been hereditary partnerships, based on the joint ownership of Hindu family law. Along with legislation providing for joint stock companies, the British introduced a new professionalism, with a far more impersonal style of management, and systems of recruitment and promotion based increasingly on seniority and merit, rather than family ties. According to Prakash Tandon, one of the first Indian executives to join a British firm, the distinction between managers and proprietors was very much a British import.

Although there was no official discrimination in favour of British business, there were obviously advantages in belonging to the ruling race in a colonial economy. 'An English firm', says Tandon, 'selling to an English government official may have had an advantage in tendering for a contract, or at least it probably enjoyed, in the eyes of the Englishman, more credibility of fulfilment of the contract.' An even more important advantage for British firms competing with new Indian ventures was that of being first in the field, as Tandon explains.

They certainly had the advantage of being better organised, better at production, and especially marketing. The old British firms, like Imperial Tobacco, or Lipton's – selling tea – or Brooke Bond or Levers, they used to have young Englishmen who would go round the countryside actually pushing their products. That's why they got known as Boxwallahs, because they carried a box of samples with them – samples of tea or textiles or anything else. They built up quite excellent marketing and distribution networks, whereas if you take the case of the Indian textile industry, all their products were sold at the factory gate. Where the British firms would go out and sell in the countryside, the Indian firms were quite content to dispose of their products at the factory site. That did give the English firms an edge and an advantage.

Prakash Tandon was one of a small but growing handful of Indians recruited into executive posts by British firms in the late 1930s. The immediate impetus came from a shortage of managerial staff caused by the enrolment of many younger British executives in the armed forces after the outbreak of the Second World War. There was also by then an awareness, at least among the more far-sighted firms, that Indian managers might be an asset in the future, given the changing political climate. The Indians chosen, however, were selected less for their business acumen than for their anglicised background, preferably a

British public school followed by Oxford or Cambridge. As Tandon discovered when he joined Lever Brothers, this could mean that they were overqualified compared with their British colleagues.

At the top, they'd decided that what they used to call 'I-sation' – Indianisation – had to begin. I remember seeing my Managing Director, and at the end of the interview I asked: 'How far can I go in this firm?' He said, very thoughtfully: 'Now that the process has begun with you, I don't see why you shouldn't be sitting in my chair one day.' So I think they made up their minds that Indianisation was a serious process. But lower down, the reactions were rather mixed, particularly as Lever's were not the kind of firm that normally went for Oxbridge or public-school types. They were more earthy salesmen from Liverpool and the provinces; and they were probably less willing to accept an Indian who was rather better educated than they were. I think I was the first professional in the firm with two or three degrees.

According to Tandon, qualifications also counted for less than colour in the eyes of Indian junior staff, accustomed to European bosses.

One afternoon, on my second or third day, I told the sepoy [office boy]: 'Can I have a cup of tea?' He said: 'No, sir. That's only for the *Sahibs*.' The *Sahibs* were naturally the Europeans. . . . And then I asked him one day: 'Could I have a towel in the toilet?' All other managers had towels with their little names on them. He said: 'No, this is also for the *Sahibs*.' Very soon my English boss realised what was happening, and he said: 'You'll get all the facilities that we get.' And the first day that my tea came on a tray, the Indian clerks and staff said: 'Well, he belongs to their class now.' And it was rather amusing to see the change in *their* attitude towards me.

Despite the entry of a few Indian executives, says Tandon, the dominant ethos of a firm like Lever's remained firmly colonial.

They had some very curious terms used in the firm. The advertising material all came from 'home'. The mail that came from England was called the 'home mail'. When I put in an expense statement for some petty cash and I signed it, the clerk came back and said: 'I'm sorry, this cannot be paid until it has a European signature.' I can only liken it to trying to become part of a herd which has been exclusive in its composition in the past. The herd instinct is to keep you out, and your instinct also is not to merge but to stay on the fringe.

According to another Indian executive, Raj Chatterji, who joined Imperial Tobacco about this time and later rose to be its Indian manager, the path to Indianisation was smoothed by the halt in British recruitment during the war years.

It was all a matter of expediency, for which the British are very well known. To quote my own example, I had exactly a year and a half of service when I was made acting branch manager of Kanpur because my boss had disappeared, joined up. They had no alternative. And they found that here were Indians, with just two or three years' experience, good enough to be left in charge of selling branches. Kanpur was one of the largest. But then, after the war, there was another batch of young Englishmen, who were with the parent company before the war and had to interrupt their careers to join up. Two of these young Englishmen were sent to me as assistants, and they were told: 'Look, you are going to serve under Indian branch managers.' I never had the slightest resentment on their side.

In the social snobbery of Anglo-India, class often counted for more than race, and this was particularly true of the business world. While Boxwallahs generally were looked down upon by ICS and army officers, there were also major social distinctions between the marketing and manufacturing sides of industry; and these applied whether you were Indian or British, as Raj Chatterji recalls.

My colleagues on the marketing side were almost without exception either straight from public school or public-school-and-university. They all came from the upper middle class. But the chaps in the factory, on the manufacturing side, had risen from the working classes, the foreman type, rough and ready. My English colleagues used to refer to them as 'the workers'. They were the gentlemen and these were the workers. . . . I didn't have much to do with the manufacturing boys; marketing people seldom did. In fact, for many years the rule was that no marketing man was allowed inside a factory, doesn't matter if he was white or brown, because manufacturing processes were considered very secret, the formula and that sort of thing. It was all wrong, because we were supposed to be selling something we knew nothing about, as far as the manufacturing of it was concerned, or what went into a cigarette. Gradually, and very sensibly, that broke down; and we were then made to go and spend some time in a factory on a secondment basis; and they came over to us. . . . They weren't too friendly to me in the beginning, because they regarded all the marketing boys as 'the toffs'; and here was a dark-skinned toff, which made it all a bit worse for them.

The oldest established section of British Indian business was the plantocracy which ran the tea, coffee and indigo industries. Plantation life, with its isolation from the European urban centres, forced them into far closer contact with the real India, represented by their workers. But they remained one of the most politically conservative sections of Anglo-Indian society; and their labour relations ranged from benevolent paternalism to conditions of near-slavery. By the 1930s, the government had introduced new legislation to protect plantation labour; but the gap between law and practice was still wide, according to Renuka Ray, the wife of an ICS officer and herself a member of the Central Legislative Assembly. She was one of a three-member panel set up by the All India Women's Conference to investigate the treatment of women labourers in the predominantly British-owned tea-gardens and collieries.

We went to some tea-gardens in Bengal and to some in Assam. And I was really quite shocked that so many of the things we had heard were so true. The treatment of women, in particular, was very bad – kicking and booting and completely destroying these women in many ways. We had decided before we went that we would not just have a conducted tour. In Assam, for instance, in one of the tea-gardens, the manager was very nice with us. We were comfortably lodged and all the rest of it. But when we suggested we'd heard a particular area was bad and we wanted to go there, he put a lot of difficulties in our way. We rather insisted on it, and we went there. And we found that the women were crying, and they came up and told us about some of the things that were happening. One woman told us that her daughter had been taken away at night, raped and then thrown back. She wanted us to go inside her hut. This the tea-garden manager did not allow us to do, but we could gather what was happening. That was one side, and the other was that they used the boot on them quite a lot.

The visitors found even worse conditions in the coal-mines; and again women suffered most. 'We went down the mines,' says Renuka Ray, 'and the conditions were horrible. The Government had signed the ILO Pact, in which no women were to be allowed underground. But when the war started, women were again sent underground.'

British managers could usually count on the local police and magistrates to keep their workers in line. But by the mid-1940s, Communist labour organisers were active in the north-eastern region, and unpopular managers had to reckon with some violent outbreaks of labour militancy. Nari Rustamji, an Indian ICS officer who served as Deputy Commissioner of the Dibrugarh tea-district in Assam, looks back on some of the most tense moments of his career.

The Communists were trying to persuade labour to really frighten the European planter. . . . And there was one planter who was on the verge of a nervous breakdown and had to be sent away and replaced. Every morning, the entire labour force went round his bungalow in procession, shouting: 'Manager *ko halal karo*' ['Slit the manager's throat']; and it was a little too much for him. We went along, and we arrested some of the ringleaders. But when we came back to our headquarters, we got a telephone-call to say that on another plantation that very same day a planter had been killed in his factory. I went there with our Superintendent of Police straight away. There was not a soul to be seen. We found our way into the factory; and then, in one corner, under one of these factory machines, we saw the body of a tall – he must have been at least six foot four – planter. He'd obviously been cringing and trying to get away beneath the machinery, and he had been hacked by the labour force. Immediately after it happened, the entire labour force went to the police station and surrendered and confessed what they had done. Here is an incident where there was a quarrel between the planter and his labour – it was quite a small matter – and they all got very excited, they hardly knew what they were doing, and they killed him. But immediately after, they made a confession to the police.

The question of Britain's long-term economic impact on India has been a vexed issue for over a century between historians of the colonial and nationalist schools. Whether one believes that the empire drained off India's wealth or that it stimulated modern commercial and industrial activity, three broad facts seem to be beyond dispute: that India's traditional manufactures declined drastically in the face of competition from machine-made British imports; that new economic activity was, at least initially, confined to the raw materials that the empire needed from India; and that neither British administrators nor entrepreneurs in India were committed to any long-term plan of economic development. Dr Ashok Mitra, one of India's leading left-wing economists, has also served as Finance Minister of West Bengal, the province where British capital first established itself. He argues that the Indian economy undoubtedly suffered a loss of potential, if not actual, wealth during the colonial period.

Over a pretty long period, if you do the sums, there is no question that there was a drainage of capital stock. I would define capital stock to include, not just the investments that were there, but the investments that *could* have taken place too. An investment which potentially could have taken place on the soil of India did not take place. And through manipulating the terms of exchange, or the terms of trade, between the goods that you sell to your imperial masters and the goods your masters sell to you, the British were able to extract a certain 'extra value' out of trade transactions, which helped their cause and harmed the Indian cause.

Mitra argues that India, like Japan, would have done far better if left to industrialise itself without colonial penetration and the distortions it brought. 'The natural process of evolution,' he says, 'from feudalism to a kind of commercial capitalism, and from commercial capitalism to full-fledged industrial capitalism, one would have expected this pattern of development to take place in India if one goes back to the middle of the eighteenth century. But the British came, they intervened, and this interrupted the process.'

Mitra also maintains that whatever development did take place under British rule was incidental to the real aims of empire.

These were really absent-minded developments. Basically, the British were interested in that kind of industrial growth in India which would help them back in Britain. For instance, they needed hessian, so they developed jute. They developed cotton textiles for the same reason. They needed cheap apparel which they could also trade in. And of course they needed the railways to transport the raw materials to the coastal areas and on to Britain by boat. . . . Along with whatever little growth took place in patches, over a very large area they promoted de-industrialisation. For instance, we do know that the Bengal apparel industry, which was quite flourishing in the seventeenth and eighteenth centuries, and even the early part of the nineteenth century, was laid to ruins by the time the nineteenth century ended. . . . The British developed the coal industry, insofar as they wanted to supplement their domestic stock of fuel from whatever they could import from India. This was again like railway development, that you develop in a manner which would help your own cause back home.

At the other end of the Indian political spectrum, M. R. Masani, a champion of private enterprise, agrees that the British attitude to Indian industry was at best half-hearted.

The textile industry in Lancashire, which supplied a great deal of cloth to India, would not have liked an indigenous Indian textile industry which supplied all of India's needs, because India was a big part of the British world market. So there's no doubt that there was a clash of national interests; and what we call protectionism today, or quotas, was being practised in reverse.

The steel industry had an interesting background. When J. N. Tata thought that India could establish a steel industry, it was considered to be quite fantastic at that time. This was in the first years of the twentieth century. He went to London to raise capital in the London money-market and got no response. And a British steel-maker made the satirical remark that, if Indians ever could produce steel, he'd eat every ton of steel that was produced in India. Within a few years, India did raise the money and produce the steel; and we used to have a joke that that particular gentleman would have died of indigestion if he had tried to eat all the steel that India managed to produce. So the British were not very friendly to Indian industrial development, rather dragged their feet. On the other hand, they were rather subtle about it. It was not very cruel or brutal.

Despite his rebuff from British financiers, J. N. Tata, a Parsi industrialist from Bombay, succeeded in establishing a business empire which remains one of India's largest and most stable. According to Sumant Moolgaokar, now one of its most senior directors, the House of Tata started as a typically Indian family concern, but used the colonial managing agency system to develop a diverse and highly professional industrial chain, ranging from hydro-electric and steel plants to soap and cosmetics. In the absence of British assistance, the Tatas turned to other European countries and found particularly enthusiastic collaborators in post-war Germany.

The present head of the House of Tata, 83-year-old J. R. D. Tata, has presided over its fortunes for half a century and is in a unique position to compare the situation of Indian business before and after independence. He remains surprisingly bitter about the colonial experience and firmly reluctant to reminisce about it. The Raj, he says, was a humiliating period in Indian history, and the sooner it is forgotten the better. Unlike many other heads of Indian business houses, he avoided social fraternising with the colonial rulers and refused to join their clubs, even though the carrot of a knighthood was dangled before him. His nationalism echoes the feelings of many Indian businessmen during the 1920s and '30s. Imperial economic control was seen as a stepmotherly regime, under which Indian business was at best ignored in the name of free enterprise and at worst subordinated to British interests by the manipulation of imperial tariffs. Pratapsinh Vissanji, for instance, still believes that Indian industry was exposed to unfair competition from Britain.

> Whichever things really competed with them, they never really encouraged or supported, although they didn't come in the way. But there were a number of hurdles, because imports were free; and one had to compete on equal terms, or you even had to be better in order to compete.... A number of industries which started at that time did face quite a lot of difficulties.... In one of the engineering firms which my father started, we had a lot of difficulty, and we ran the business at a loss for nineteen years, because we were facing very stiff competition both from imports and the British engineering companies working in India.

Sumant Moolgaokar, who started as an executive in the cement industry in 1930, adds that the lack of British support led many new firms to set up in the princely states, which offered more incentives than British India.

> In those days, the cement factories were only in the Indian states, not in the India under the British Raj. That was because there was no taxation whatsoever in the Indian states, and they encouraged the setting up of industrial units more than the British government. Neither was there any protection: imported cement was freely allowed. At a time when the cement industry was growing, one would have expected a little protection. But many cement units went into liquidation because there was no protection whatsoever.

By the 1920s, the Raj, under intense political pressure from Indian nationalism, did start to move in a more interventionist and protectionist direction. Tariffs against imports, though still very light, were introduced; and a series of policy-papers called for more active industrialisation. The result, according to Prakash Tandon, was that by the late 1930s some sections of Indian industry were becoming strong enough to mount a serious challenge to British producers.

Indian exports were becoming competitive. Take the interesting example of textiles. In the 1930s, the British textile industry was seeking protection against the Indian textile industry. There was a large, high-level mission that went to England to negotiate the terms of the textile trade between Lancashire and India, so as to make sure that Indian competition didn't push the British textiles too hard.

The new assertiveness of Indian business was expressed politically in open support for Gandhi's *Swadeshi* (literally 'From your own country') campaign, with its semi-religious boycott of foreign goods. Ashok Mitra sees the Mahatma's appeal to economic nationalism as a political master-stroke.

> The old gentleman was a sly fox. . . . He knew that if he was to succeed in confronting the British, he must have a wide mass base. At the same time, he must have the support of indigenous Indian capital. And he thought this was one idea which would capture the imagination of both – the local bourgeoisie as much as the popular masses. You appeal to the nationalism of the masses by *Swadeshi*, and through buying *Swadeshi* you also help the cause of Indian capital.

This may explain why even a family like the Vissanjis, with their long-standing British business connections, was swept into Gandhi's movement. Pratapsinh Vissanji describes how his father dealt with this conflict of loyalties.

> My father always believed in *Swadeshi*, and he said that things which could be manufactured in this country, why should they be imported, because it would also give employment and help the country. So he was one of the co-sponsors of the *Swadeshi* movement. . . . Of course, it did have a certain amount of impact on our business relationships; but by and large, the British partners were very fair-minded and they never objected to this. They knew my father's views; and they knew that we were helping the *Swedeshi* movement and that we were also for the independence of India.

With the growing popularity of *Swadeshi*, the days when even the cast-iron manhole covers for the sewers were British-made and imported were clearly numbered. The Second World War gave a major boost to this process by emphasising the need for a more self-reliant economy and by making India an important production base for British war supplies, as Prakash Tandon explains.

> Through the 1940s, we had an excellent opportunity for diversification of industry, because imports had tailed off. . . . Also, the British government was making heavy purchases in India, because in this part of the world India was the only country with an industrial, engineering capacity, more than Ceylon or Burma or

Malaya. They had to depend heavily on Indian manufactures of one kind or another, be they uniforms or light weapons or engineering or bridging goods. By 1945, the Indian economy was an established, reasonably diversified thing.

Sumant Moolgaokar, with his experience of the earlier difficulties of the cement industry, describes how the needs of war production changed the Government's *laissez-faire* attitude to Indian business.

I was looking after the expansion in the cement industry. In 1944, I was called by the Director-General of Supplies, and they wanted us to put up a cement factory for the Burma front. They gave us all the assistance, and we put up that factory. We made quite a lot of the heavy equipment here in India; and we imported the power plant and things that were not available here. They saw to it that we were able to put up the factory in two years.

The expansion and diversification of Indian industry during the War had set the stage for the great industrial leap which would follow independence. Yet such growth would have been inconceivable in peacetime under a colonial government whose economic philosophy remained tinged with its early trading origins and with Victorian principles of *laissez-faire*.

The most disappointing feature of India's economic development under the Raj was that industrialisation was not accompanied by any significant agrarian changes. Indian agriculture remained primitive and unproductive, based on an antiquated, feudal system of land tenure, artificially buttressed by the colonial rulers. Ashok Mitra offers some clues to the agrarian conservatism of the Raj.

It could be the difficulties they faced in the initial years of empire in trying to involve themselves too closely with developments in the countryside; or it could be that they were baffled by 1857 and all that took place during that year. But they adopted a policy of withdrawing from direct administration and decided that they would operate through commission-agents, landlords or *zamindars* in the countryside. They would extract a small rental from the commission-agent and leave him to plunder the countryside. As a consequence, the development of infrastructure in agriculture was completely neglected, apart from the fact that no scientific tenurial arrangements could be experimented with; and both severely affected agricultural production and productivity.

Despite the zeal of individual district officers, British administration in rural India brought few social or economic improvements. Instead, the Raj pinned its hopes on the urban middle classes, through whom progress was expected to filter down to the rural masses. But the middle classes themselves remained disgruntled and frustrated by the slow pace of industrialisation and the very limited employment prospects that this implied. By the 1920s, thousands of educated Indians were emerging from higher education to find that there were no jobs for them, either in the government services or in the private sector. The success of a chosen few who were making it into executive positions via Oxbridge was little consolation. Like Indian businessmen, unemployed youth blamed the economic shackles of the Raj and British capital for India's economic ills. It was this convergence of economic interests which formed the basis of the nationalist movement.

SPREADING THE WORD

Our editorial style was certainly distinctive. What distinguished us from other newspapers in India was this very strong feeling of the integrity of editorial opinions being respected. In the old days, the chairman of Andrew Yule kept a kind of fatherly eye on The Statesman's *affairs, and consultations did take place between the editor and the chairman of Andrew Yule. But at no stage was there any suggestion about what the newspaper should say; and that has been respected ever since.*

C. R. Irani (Managing Director, The Statesman, Calcutta)

Along with the English language and Western education, India's nineteenth-century British rulers introduced the printing press. Its role initially was to produce English-language textbooks; but it expanded rapidly in the hands of Christian missionaries eager to popularise the Gospel; and it was later adopted by Indian reformers and educationists as the instrument of their own cultural renaissance. Printing was a powerful stimulus to the revival of India's vernacular languages and literature. But while the vernacular press was Indian-owned, the English-language press and the political power it controlled remained till the end of empire a near-total British monopoly.

By the late nineteenth century, the press in India included a network of English-language newspapers, covering virtually every major city in British India. With few exceptions, they were British-owned and managed, founded by boxwallahs, missionaries and retired civil servants. Yet, they were not mere mouthpieces of colonial rule. At a time when government was free of any parliamentary accountability, some eminent papers acted as a major check on authoritarian rule. One example is *The Statesman* of Calcutta, which remains one of India's leading national dailies and an outspoken critic of government.

The present Managing Director of *The Statesman*, Cusrow Irani, is proud of his paper's colonial origins. It was the child of a partnership between two eminent nineteenth-century Britons. One was Robert Knight, an unconventional ICS officer, who felt that Indian public opinion was not being adequately represented in the existing press. He merged two other papers to form *The Statesman* and became its first editor. He was assisted by William Carey, a missionary and educationist, who lived in a princely state outside British India because he believed that colonial rule did not allow sufficient freedom of speech. His favourite chair, with its large and stately Victorian proportions, still graces the *Statesman* boardroom, rescued from a dusty cellar by a clerk with a sense of history.

44

The owners of *The Statesman* were the Yule family in Britain, whose business interests were represented by one of Calcutta's leading managing agency houses, Andrew Yule. But according to Irani, the proprietors never interfered with editorial independence: 'It's a tribute, I think, to the form of ownership that, until the early sixties, when the last of the Yule family died out, the paper continued to be owned by that family and betrayed no signs of its ownership in its editorial columns or in its news coverage.'

Although *The Statesman* had a reputation for conservatism in nationalist circles, its editorial policy was often critical of government as well. Irani describes the role played by Ian Stephens, a British editor in the 1940s.

He was editor here during the 1942 Bengal famine. And he, a British editor of a then British-owned newspaper, was thundering away, demanding that the Famine Code be declared. The British government would not listen. He then had a visiting card prepared with his name on one side and, on the other, four reproductions of the most gruesome deaths on the streets of Calcutta. He took a train to Delhi with three hundred of these cards and made sure that every senior government official got this token from him. The point was taken; the Famine Code was declared. And years later, in 1975, during our centenary year, when we invited Ian Stephens to come to Calcutta, he had a very emotional welcome from total strangers on the streets of Calcutta – some of the old-timers – who recognised him and said: 'Are you Ian Stephens, the editor? Thank you for what you did for Bengal!'

British-owned papers like *The Statesman* in Calcutta and the *Times of India* in Bombay were by no means pro-independence. But by upholding editorial freedom and demonstrating the political power of an autonomous press, they acted as a catalyst and a model for several nationalist dailies that sprang up in their wake. Some were launched by Congress leaders as vehicles for their campaigns and floundered under a combination of government censorship and financial troubles. But two of the most successful remain in the top league of the Indian press – the *Indian Express*, founded in Madras, and the *Amrita Bazaar Patrika*, based in Calcutta.

The *Amrita Bazaar Patrika* was founded as a Bengali-language paper, strongly committed to the Congress cause; and it was an accident of censorship that drove it to launch an English edition. Toshar Kanti Ghosh, the 88-year-old proprietor of what is now a large newspaper chain, delights in describing how his father, the paper's founder, overcame British efforts to suppress it in the 1880s. He was sent for by the then Governor of Bengal, Sir Ashley Eden, and asked if he would allow the Governor to see his editorials before publication. Recognising this as a form of pre-censorship, he first pleaded that it would be impossible because of the delays involved. When the Governor insisted, he asked: 'Do you not want that there should be at least one honest newspaper in the country?' An enraged Eden terminated the interview with a threat to drive Ghosh out of Calcutta in six months. The result was a Vernacular Press Act, which made government vetting a legal requirement for all vernacular-language papers. But the *Amrita Bazaar Patrika* circumvented the Act by converting itself into an English-language paper, despite the financial odds. During the following half-century up to independence, and after, it remained staunchly pro-Congress; and although government censors made many attempts to close it down with punitive fines, public donations kept the paper going.

Despite the commercial success and political influence of some Indian-owned newspapers, their journalists never enjoyed the status and prestige of their counterparts in the British-owned press. Romesh Thapar was one of the few Indians to join the editorial staff of a British paper, the *Times of India*, and he describes what a privileged position this was in the 1940s.

> In those days, the freedom struggle was on, and the journalist was meeting everyone who was a party to the drama, so he was looked up to. We were all on leading committees, even brains-trusts, because we were very well informed. . . . It was extremely prestigious to be an assistant editor with the *Times of India*. It was the way the whole society looked at you. I remember, during the war years, whenever we needed a bottle of whiskey, which was very difficult to get, one used to just send a note down to the local booze-shop and sign 'R. Thapar, Assistant Editor', and bang, it came! Nobody resisted that kind of letter. We were much honoured, and it was a very discriminatory society.

In the world of journalism, as in business, young Indian recruits encountered some of the legacies of European monopoly, such as whites-only toilets. But once such hurdles had been overcome, they usually entered into a far more equal and creative relationship with British seniors than would have been possible in government service. Romesh Thapar, for instance, found Sir Francis Lowe, the British editor of the *Times of India*, remarkably tolerant of his nationalist and even Communist affiliations.

> He was quite a remarkable person. He used to hold an editorial conference every morning. He had been through the entire paper, marked all the errors in red pencil. Everyone was responsible for a page. And when it came to deciding what editorials had to be written, he'd turn round and ask us: 'Tell me, Thapar, what's this going on in the Punjab? What do you think about it?' I used to tell him very frankly. If it agreed with his notions, he said: 'You do the piece.' If it didn't agree, he'd say: 'Well, that's interesting. I'll be writing that.' It was one way of never getting us to write against what we believed. It was a very sensitive way of handling us.

This liberal approach made it possible for a left-wing journalist like Thapar to remain politically active while working for the *Times* and to pass on useful information to politicians outside. When the British Communist, R. Palme Dutt, regarded as a dangerous revolutionary by the Raj, visited India to collect material for a book, Thapar was able to open his home to the controversial visitor with no more hindrance than a humorous exchange with his editor.

When Palme Dutt visited India, the Communist Party didn't know where to put him. So they came to us and said: 'He'll stay with you.' We said 'OK.' I walked into the office three days after Palme Dutt had arrived, and Francis Lowe turned to me and said: 'You know, the London *Times* is telling me that there's a Communist rabble-rouser in India and I've got to locate the man. Now you have contacts. Could you tell me where this man is?' I said: 'He's staying in my house!' 'Good God,' he said, 'they say he's going to paralyse India with a railway strike!' I said: 'No, he's just doing a revision of *India Today*.'

Francis Lowe's benevolence extended beyond editorial matters to the domestic welfare of his Indian assistants. When Thapar wanted to marry, Sir Francis, in a display of British paternalism at its best, did all he could to smooth the path financially.

One day I told him: 'I'm thinking of getting married, but I can't on this salary.' So he looked at me and, first question, which was always very important to the Brits in India: 'Who are you marrying?' I told him. 'Oh yes,' he said, 'I know her father. All right. You come over on Thursday, and Lady Lowe will discuss what is to be done.' And there I was in my dinner-jacket, going for a formal, little dinner with the Lowes. We sat down and talked about the world and everything; and after dinner, she sat down with some paper and said: 'Now, let's plan the budget!' I used to get the great sum of 400 rupees[1] a month in those days as assistant editor, a lot of money, actually, because it was 4000 rupees a month by today's standards, and I was only 22. She made a budget, and Sir Francis looked at it and said: 'Yes, that seems good enough.' It was more than double what I was getting, 900 rupees. And he said: 'We'll sanction that with retrospective effect from January, because you'll need to have some money to equip your flat, etc.'

Sir Francis Lowe was, by all accounts, an unusually liberal editor. But the proprietors of the *Times of India* also tolerated Thapar's left-wing connections and even took a polite interest in his stage appearances with the pro-Communist People's Theatre.

I used to normally send them all the pre-publicity. The entire Board of the *Times of India* used to sit in the front row on opening night and witness the sort of plays we used to put on, like *Waiting for Lefty* – real strike-action stuff, which was localised to the Indian scene and made fun of the British. And they all came and religiously

---

1 Ten rupees were then equivalent to a pound sterling.

sat there, five of them. They never passed a comment, but always came to see what I was doing.

By far the most unconventional member of British India's intellectual establishment was a former BBC man, Lionel Fielden, who came out to India in 1936 to establish a state broadcasting service. The Government was by now aware of the tremendous political and educational potential of broadcasting and had decided to replace the few existing private radio stations with a single, national network in its own hands. The choice of a maverick like Fielden to head the new enterprise was surprising. It seems that he was appointed in London, on the recommendation of the BBC's presiding deity, Lord Reith; and the bureaucracy in India did not quite realise what they were getting.

Fielden set about recruiting a talented group of young Indians to run the new service. His methods of selection were refreshingly unorthodox. He met people informally, sized them up and offered them a job if he thought they were up to it. Neither sex nor political leanings were a disqualification in Fielden's eyes. One of his most successful appointments was Miss Mehra Masani, then a young sociology graduate from the London School of Economics, who became Deputy Director-General of All India Radio after independence and remains the doyenne of Indian broadcasting. She says that Fielden first approached her brother, M. R. Masani, then a prominent left-wing politician. Masani refused to have anything to do with a government organisation, but suggested Fielden try his sister instead. He did; they got on well, and she took the job. She remembers Fielden as the founder of all that is best in Indian broadcasting.

> He was an extraordinary man, a rolling stone undoubtedly, a man of exceptional intelligence, a very versatile intellect, interested in a large number of things. But I suppose people with a very strictly disciplined, academic mind might have found him somewhat wild. He would have brilliant ideas, but was not always able to put them through because of a certain lack of discipline. He was an extremely tall, handsome Englishman with a mane of grey hair and exceedingly charming. He made friends with anybody that he wanted to. He was very popular with all the Indians that he ever came across; and, of course, that was his undoing as far as the British establishment was concerned. He was some kind of distant relation of Lord Linlithgow, who was then the Viceroy. And Linlithgow resented Fielden even more because of that. He felt he was letting the side down, hobnobbing with people like Nehru and his sister, Vijayalakshmi Pandit, and making friends with people like my brother, people who were certainly a bad lot from the British point of view. But, of course, this made him exceedingly popular with his Indian staff.

Left to himself, Fielden would have liked to make Indian broadcasting genuinely representative of the prevailing political climate, offering airtime to nationalist leaders. Mehra Masani describes the tussles this involved with the bureaucracy.

> What did one do about Gandhi? Lionel, of course, would have liked to put him on the air, but he was told he couldn't. That led to quite a long argument in files and in meetings; but Lionel never succeeded in bringing Gandhi to the microphone while he was there. He did get Sarojini Naidu[1] to come and talk about Gandhi, because it was an amusing sort of talk. She called him 'a little Mickey-Mouse of a man', and the establishment obviously thought it was harmless, so it wouldn't really matter very much. He wasn't made out to be a great saint or a great patriot. . . . But more or less every day there would be friction over some thing or other, not only political, also administrative. They would object to Lionel's somewhat free and easy way of doing things. They felt he was not sufficiently careful about rules and regulations and procedures and accounts. And he would say: 'I'm concerned with broadcasting. I'm not concerned with all these pettyfogging details.' That was a point of view which could not commend itself to the establishment.

Although he never managed to get Gandhi on air, Fielden, according to Mehra Masani, did outmanoeuvre the bureaucracy by getting the new network named All India Radio.

> It was the perfect name, because the initials spelled 'AIR', and it gave the proper picture of an All India service. But he said to persuade the bureaucracy to have accepted this would have been extremely difficult. They wanted 'Indian State Broadcasting Service', which was what it was called at the time. So he thought it would have to be planted and we would have to pretend that one of *them* had thought of it; and who better than the Viceroy? So, walking one day in the garden of Viceregal House, he said to Linlithgow: 'A good name must be found for this Indian State Broadcasting Service. It's a horribly dull sort of name.' And Linlithgow said: 'Yes, well. . . .' So he said: 'First, we've got to think of the whole of India.' Linlithgow said: 'Well, All India, obviously.' Lionel said: 'Yes, that's right, All India. Then you've got to bring radio into it somehow, because after all that's what the service is about.' So Linlithgow said: 'Yes, why not All India Radio?' Lionel said: 'That's the perfect name! Thank you so much, Your Excellency!'

Fielden left India soon after the outbreak of the Second World War, knowing that he would find it impossible to survive the tight censorship to which wartime broadcasting was subjected. Although his stay in India was brief, his imprint on All India Radio proved indelible, whether in the commitment to autonomy which Mehra Masani and his other protegés inherited or in more mundane details of interior design and decoration.

---

1 Poetess and veteran nationalist leader, Sarojini Naidu, one of Gandhi's closest aides, is perhaps best remembered for her irreverent sense of humour.

He went into every little detail of the planning of studios. When I joined the Bombay station, we were in a building in the commercial area of Bombay and had to shut windows and doors whenever a broadcast was going on; and in spite of that, motor-car noises would drift in. But soon our new studios were ready in a much better part of town. And I was quite amazed at the samples of curtain material that he'd collect for insulating sound, and the design on the sellotex which was used for sound-proofing, and the carpet which was to be used in the talks studio as distinct from the drama studio. We learnt a good deal from Lionel in these matters; and every set of studios that came up after that would copy this kind of design, with the result that our studios were always extremely pleasant and much admired.

Lord Reith came through in the 1950s, and I had the honour of showing him round Broadcasting House. He said: 'They are very well-planned and well-devised studios.' And I said: 'It was Lionel Fielden who did that.' Although he wasn't there when the building was ready, he was the one who had planned Broadcasting House. Reith was very pleased with this, because Lionel had been his choice to come to India and run broadcasting here.

Journalists like Fielden, Francis Lowe and Ian Stephens built bridges between Britons and Indians that have survived long after independence; and there were others like them in the world of education. But unfortunately, liberal intellectuals were always a drop in the ocean of bureaucracy and commercialism that made up traditional Anglo-India. And it was the prejudices of the bureaucrats and boxwallahs that determined the social and cultural meeting of the races in British India.

JOINING THE CLUB

There was this dance on Independence Eve at the Cawnpore Club,
which until two years before had been an entirely British club. It
was one of the oldest clubs in India, founded in 1888. It was really
a preserve of the British boxwallah. . . . But on that night, here
were these British burra sahibs[1] *dancing with Indians and vice*
versa. It was a rather touching occasion. Precisely at midnight, the
whole thing came to a halt, and the club band played 'God Save the
King' for the last time. The Union Jack was lowered from the club
ballroom, and the Indian flag went up; and the band tried to play
the Indian national anthem. They played it after a fashion; and
there was this hand-clapping and kissing and hugging all round,
Indian and European.

Raj Chatterji (former executive, Imperial Tobacco)

Raj Chatterji is one of a small and dwindling band of Indian 'survivors' who grew up under the Raj, received an Oxbridge education and remain unashamedly anglophile in their accents and lifestyle. But the camaraderie he describes between the British and Indians would have been rare in the heyday of the Raj. Clubs were the social hub of empire; but, with few exceptions, they kept out Indians. The Cawnpore Club – steeped in memories of the Mutiny, when Cawnpore (now Kanpur) was the scene of a major massacre of British civilians – was one of the strictest in its exclusion of Indians. But there were many others up and down the country where an Indian could not enter, even if he happened to be a Maharaja invited to dinner by a British Governor. The Royal Bombay Yacht Club was one of them. Dorothy Ganapathy, another Indian 'survivor', to whom Paul Scott dedicated his Raj Quartet, tells the well-known tale of how Lord Willingdon, then Governor of Bombay, and later Viceroy, rebelled against such prejudice.

He invited four or five Maharajas to the Yacht Club for dinner. When their cars drew up, they were not allowed to enter; so they were all outside. Lord Willingdon came down and said: 'Where are my guests? It's now coming on to nine o'clock.' And they said: 'Indians are not allowed.' So he came out and said: 'I'm sorry.' And he then and there wrote his resignation from the Yacht Club. He collected whatever food he could – he was Governor after all – and they went to Government House and had dinner. And that day they sat down and decided to form a club. Lord Willingdon said: 'Yes, for Indians only.' And all the Maharajas, who gave a lot of money,

1 Bosses.

said: 'No, we're not vindictive. It's for everybody.' And that's how it was called the Willingdon Club. It was the first club that Indians and Europeans could go to and mix.

Other mixed clubs, like the Roshanara Club in Delhi, followed the Willingdon. Yet, even at these places, the mixing of races remained halting and limited. British and Indian colleagues might take a drink together or even share a game of golf or tennis, but more intimate social contact was rare, as Khushwant Singh explains.

My father was among the few black members of the Delhi Gymkhana Club. This was only for show; Indians who had been knighted were regarded as wogs acceptable to the British. But the Gymkhana Club and other clubs which started taking Indians made conditions very difficult. You had to be interviewed. Your wife had to be there with you. Now my mother couldn't speak a word of English. They invited you to cocktail dances. She didn't take any drink at the time; and she would certainly have been absolutely appalled if she'd had to dance on the floor. They made a few exceptions, but no young Indians were ever accepted as members in those clubs; so the contacts were only business contacts.

The British, according to Raj Chatterji, blamed the social mores of Indians, most of whom left their wives at home and laid themselves open to the charge that they were operating a double standard.

Although some of our chaps were from westernised families, they weren't westernised to the point of bringing out their wives. So the Englishmen felt it was pretty hard going socialising with a chap whose wife can hardly speak English or only comes in to say 'Good morning, good evening' and disappears. And the same thing in the clubs: 'Why should the Indians come and ogle our women when leaving their own wives at home?' . . . The trouble was that, apart from people like my mother, who was a very keen bridge-player and played tennis, I can't remember more than about two Indian women who regularly attended the club. The British would bring their womenfolk sometimes; but then they said: 'It's more or less a men's club as far as we're concerned, because Indians are not here with their wives.' So their more intimate parties were always held either at the Delhi Club or in their own homes.

Whites-only places like the Delhi Club remained a symbolic reminder of the alien and humiliating side of foreign rule. The last of them, the Breach Candy Swimming Pool in Bombay, excluded Indians till the 1960s and continues to operate discriminatory entry rules for visitors.

The vast majority of Indians, of course, had no desire to enter European society. And the notion of ethnic segregation was by no means new in a caste-ridden society where many Brahmins would still not eat food touched by lower castes. What made Anglo-Indian racism unacceptable was that it was practised by foreign rulers and affected precisely those Indians who were most westernised and had the strongest aspirations to equality. As Dorothy Ganapathy explains, there was something particularly galling about a system which allowed in the most humble white, but excluded the most aristocratic Indian. Mrs Ganapathy was the daughter of an eminent political figure, Sir Hari Singh Gaur, Leader of the Opposition in the Central Legislative Assembly. She was also one of the few Indian women of her generation to travel to England as a student in the 1930s, returning with a degree from Durham University. Her husband was a colonel in the Indian Medical Service (IMS); but they could not enter the local club where his colleagues went, even though the most down-at-heel travelling salesman could go there if he was British.

> Quite a few Britishers in Madras, both in the IMS and ICS, were dead against this – that we of our birth and education were not allowed to come into the clubs, but met in one another's houses. People who came selling toilet-paper and toothbrushes were allowed to come in; but we were not allowed.

Mrs Ganapathy describes with relish how she ventured to expose the absurdity of entry rules at one of the most exclusive places in British India, the Adyar Club in Madras.

> A gentleman from Turkey came to stay with us. And the Surgeon-General, General Wilson, invited him to the Adyar Club for dinner. So I told him: 'You can't go bare-headed. After all, it's such a big club. Wear your fez cap.' So he wore a huge *tarbush* with a big tassel hanging. When he got to the Adyar Club, the Indian peon who opened the door said: 'No, you can't enter. Coloured people are not allowed.' When he came back, I asked: 'How did you like the dinner?' He said: 'I was not admitted.' I said: 'Oh, why not?' And he said: 'I had on what you told me to wear.' The next day, General Wilson came to lunch and he said: 'Why did you do that?' I said: 'Well, General, I didn't think that he would be refused. After all, Turkey is in Europe and you allow in Europeans.' He laughed.

There was a time, before the Raj established itself, when Europeans and Indians had mixed freely. The soldiers of fortune who conquered India for the East India Company may have plundered and looted, but many of them also acquired Indian languages and learning, took on the manners of the local nobility and settled down with Indian wives. By Victorian times, all this was scorned as going native. But echoes of a more liberal past lingered on, not least in relations between the sexes. For instance, as Nari Rustamji recalls, British planters in Assam, despite their reputation for racial arrogance, commonly kept Indian mistresses.

> When a young planter came to this remote place, he had his physical urges, like any young man would have, and he might keep somebody for some time, because I don't think they were allowed to get married for the first few years of their service on the tea-

plantation. Then, after a few years, he would go back to England, acquire a wife and come back; and the other lady would be usually fairly suitably pensioned off. That was a recognised arrangement which had been going on for scores and scores of years. Nobody thought very much about it.

Even senior members of the exclusive ICS were not above such liaisons, though, as Raj Chatterji describes, they might go to absurd lengths to keep up appearances.

There was the famous story of this ICS man. He was a judge, I think. Everyone knew that he had this Indian mistress, but no one did anything about it. If his colleagues called, she was at the back of the house. Whenever he was transferred, he'd solve the problem by having a huge wooden box made, ostensibly to carry a piano. But he had little holes made in it, and inside was a nice little mattress and pillow and all that. And this girlfriend of his would be the piano. So it was well known that the Judge Sahib never travelled without his piano; and it was accepted by both Europeans and Indians.

But, as Rustamji reminds us, such secret romances could sometimes end in tragedy.

I knew an ICS officer who had a mistress; and she committed suicide in his bungalow, which naturally caused a lot of tension at that time. . . . She stayed with him, and she was very possessive. When he went out on tour, she suspected that he was probably living with another girl. And when he came back, he found that she had hanged herself in the bathroom.

While the Raj tolerated discreet relations between British men and Indian women, similar contact between white women and Indian men was strictly taboo. There were a few Indians who acquired British wives, usually while they were students in Britain; but these unfortunate women were generally treated as outcasts by both British and Indian society, dismissed collectively as 'barmaids'. There were also occasional instances when a mem-sahib proper broke ranks. Raj Chatterji remembers a *cause célèbre* when an Indian ICS officer had a passionate affair with the wife of a British colleague. Ironically, when their secret was discovered, it was her husband who was penalised and not her lover. He was held responsible for his wife's misconduct and transferred to another district. 'There must have been quite a few Englishwomen,' Chatterji muses, 'who were attracted by Indians – the refined type of Indian who'd mix with them on equal terms. But there was that inhibition that she could go only so far and not the whole hog. There'd be a mild flirtation perhaps, at the most, except for the rare case.'

For Indians of a younger generation, growing up in the 1920s and 1930s, the sexual apartheid of the Raj appeared offensive and anachronistic. Khushwant Singh, a westernised Sikh who went to university in England, describes his feelings when he discovered that white women were out of bounds in India: 'If there was some very plain-looking Englishwoman, who couldn't find a white husband, she might deign to have an affair with an Indian, and perhaps end up by marrying him. It was very difficult for people like me who'd been educated in England, when coming back here you could hardly talk to young English girls. They kept their distance from us.'

Fear of scandal, and a deep-seated racial paranoia about Indian men as would-be rapists or seducers, made even the most innocent contact between British women and Indian men enormously complicated. Raj Chatterji describes how, as late as 1940, a British colleague would not have dreamt of leaving his wife alone in the house with him.

> I was a Junior Assistant in Cawnpore, and the British branch manager in a small place called Dalsingh Serai in north Bihar was a member of the AIRO [Army in India Reserve of Officers] and had to go for his annual training camp. Because of the depletion caused by the war, he was there by himself, living in this very luxurious bungalow out in the wilds. He'd just got married and brought his wife out; so I was sent to look after the ranch while he was away. I was the first Indian I think that he'd ever found staying in his bungalow. . . . They were both very kind, and we got on exceedingly well. A very pretty girl, this wife of his; and I was wondering what was going to happen when he went on his fifteen days' leave, wondering and hoping. Now, they were rather fond of cats, and they had a cat called Sheba who always joined us over the evening drink, sitting and purring away in her mistress's very delectable lap. The night before the man was due to leave, he said to me: 'I say, old boy, I hope you won't mind looking after her.' I said: 'Not at all, my dear chap, with great pleasure. After all, she's your wife.' He said: 'Wife! I was talking about Sheba, the cat.' And it transpired that the wife went with him, and he left her somewhere with some British friends.

The British *mem-sahib* or wife, with her ignorance and suspicion of all things Indian, was the person most commonly blamed for the breakdown in relations between the races. Bound hand and foot by the social and sexual conventions of male Anglo-India, most mem-sahibs certainly had neither the opportunity nor the curiosity to explore the real India. Renuka Ray, who was married to an Indian ICS officer, explains why she avoided her British counterparts.

> I did go to the club, and I knew how to play tennis and bridge and all the rest of it. But I could not tolerate some of the things they started saying, and I used to have long and bitter discussions with them. Eventually, I decided it was better for me not to meet them too much, because they didn't like me. . . . British mem-sahibs in India – and there were certainly notable exceptions – were people who had little conception of what was happening in the country.

They lived in a very closed circle, went to the club and probably played tennis and things. . . . How they could close their eyes, I don't know, but I used to marvel at it – how they didn't see what was in front of them, the misery of the people when the famines were on and things like that.

When there was relief work to be done, I was interested, and I used to work in the districts. I remember that someone came to see me because I was an Indian ICS officer's wife; and while she was there, people came round who had to be helped and others who were helping them. She saw this, and I told her that I thought she would take an interest. Her reply was: 'Don't you think you might get some disease if you mix too much with these people?' They were so immersed in keeping everything hygienic and clean in their homes. Every day they changed all the *jharans* [dusters]. They always had their servants use gloves before they served at table and things like that which irritated me considerably.'

Another Indian woman, Dorothy Ganapathy, claims that the arrogance of British mem-sahibs stemmed often from their own lack of breeding and education.

They didn't come from very good families at all. They married for the sake of marrying, I suppose, and companionship. And they became very haughty. They had dozens of servants, though they never had one servant in England; and they thought every one of us was servant class. . . . I remember once at a gathering one Englishwoman turned to me and said: 'Oh, what beautiful English you talk.' I said: 'Really? I'm surprised you acknowledge it. After all, we educated Indians talk English all the time. Thank you for noticing, but it's not a compliment.'

Underlying the isolation of the sahibs and mem-sahibs was a fear, not only of disease, but that too much familiarity with the natives might breed contempt; and this could apply to the most westernised and upper-class Indians. Many who went to England as students were surprised to find how much friendlier the British were on their home ground. Harindranath Chattopadhyaya, an 88-year-old poet and veteran of the nationalist movement, was one of the first batch of Indian students to gain admission to Cambridge in the years before the First World War. He describes how he was adopted by a British shopkeeper and his family while on vacation in London.

He had a tea-stall specially for bus-drivers. . . . When I went there, I said: 'May I have a cup of tea please, sir?' He said: 'My son, of course, here you are.' He poured me out a lovely cup of tea, delicious, and when I went to pay for it, he said: 'No, I'm not going to take anything from you. You are my son, my Indian son, a first son from India. Where are you staying?' I said: 'Well, I've got no place really to stay.' 'Oh, come and share our home,' he said. I was very grateful, and in the evening he took me to his place. . . . I stayed there. And there was his daughter, Rosie, tall woman, who called me 'my Indian brother'. They received me with so much warmth, I was actually floored. They were wonderful people.

Govind Swaminathan, a barrister who went to public school and university in England, also made close friends there. But he discovered on his return journey to India the literal truth of the saying that the Englishman east of Suez became a very different person.

On the boat, I had made friends with an Englishman, a young man of my age group, about 21 or 22. After Port Said, he had a very worried look, so I said to him: 'Something seems to be troubling you.' He said: 'Yes, last night those senior chaps got hold of me, and they said: "Look, we're just telling you this for your own good, that when you get to Calcutta and take up this job, you mustn't be very friendly with Indians. And we notice that you're very friendly with this young Indian. Now, he might have been at Oxford and the rest of it, but still you had better be careful." ' I found the Englishman in India was so totally different from the Englishman in England, with whom I'd been at school and at university.

Rajeshwar Dayal, an Indian ICS officer, recalls that his Cambridge-educated wife had a similar experience.

She had some women friends at Newnham and Girton, and one of them was married to a young ICS officer. They travelled to India by the same boat. But once they arrived in India, there was no social contact between them whatsoever – a very strange thing.

Not all Indians, it must be said, were that eager to mix with Europeans, especially those whom they regarded as being not quite out of 'the top-drawer'. Tara Ali Baig, who grew up in a conservative district of Bengal, says that the British were often blissfully unaware of the scorn with which they were regarded by the old, native aristocracy.

We were certainly snobs too. A great many English people who came out in different jobs, whether it was as businessmen or as technical people, they were very varied in their level. Some people were definitely upper class, what you might call the top-drawer, but there were a lot of others who were not. The interesting thing was the snobbery that there was between themselves, as well as between them and the upper-class Indian, who looked upon them as something they had to endure, but didn't necessarily have to fraternise with.

It was particularly visible, for instance, in the big *zamindari* families, the landed gentry of Bengal, where there was a tremendous snobbery, in that they would not have anyone come to their house who did not have certain family qualifications. But where it was oftentimes hilarious was when the high official's wife, who may not have been all that top-drawer herself, wanted to call on one of these ladies. There was a great flutter in the *zamindari*

house . . . and the kind of comments that there were between the
Indian ladies when the Britishers had left, and among the British
women when they were getting into their various cars, was often
hilarious. The Indian women would say: 'What sort of people are
these? Their dress is so vulgar; they expose their legs. Look at those
white arms; they look as if they haven't been cooked. And why do
they wear those peculiar things on their heads?' And the British
women would leave the place saying: 'Really, isn't it shocking,
these women are so backward. Did you see that they didn't even
know how to drink from a cup?' There was all this kind of banter
that would go on between the two sides.

European society, too, was always as class-conscious as it was
racialist; and as Govind Swaminathan explains, being an upper-class,
Oxbridge-educated Indian could give one advantages over a British
businessman.

I was able to spot what class they came from by their accent in
English – I mean the aitches being dropped and cockney and all
that – which didn't make me popular. There were three of us, all
from the same school in England. One was an ADC to the
Governor, so he was, I suppose, in their top-bracket. Another was
in business, a boxwallah as he was called. Now, normally the
boxwallah and the ADC should have been particularly good friends
here. They'd been in the same house at school at the same time. But
they never used to talk to each other; and the only way they used to
communicate with each other was through me. My mother used to
have fantastic tennis-parties, and there used to be a kind of thing
that you'd arrived in Madras society when you were asked to Mrs
Swaminathan's tennis-party. She used to have a mixture of her
Indian friends and my friends, these boys who were at school with
me. And you should have seen the way they behaved towards each
other – they never talked to each other when they were here. So I
realised that you might talk about our caste system, but this British
class system was terrible.

Even if they dropped their aitches, the sahibs were still courted by
Indians who had what was called 'a white-skin-complex'. Khushwant
Singh, whose father was an ardent loyalist, knighted for his services,
remembers how trying the meeting of East and West was for the rest of
the family.

My father, being a builder, came into contact with English
engineers and architects and, occasionally, called on them on
Christmas Day and New Year's Day to give presents and keep them
on the right side. If he was able to persuade them ever to accept
hospitality, it was a nightmare, because the arrangements had to be
made and a band had to be brought. We had to get caterers from
outside, like Wenger's or Davico's, to do the catering. None of our
servants could cope with it. . . . Everything was vastly exaggerated;

Above: *Lord Clive, the founder of British colonial power in India, being granted the Diwani (revenue administration) of Bengal by the Mughal emperor, Shah Alam, in 1765. The East India Company maintained that empire was thrust upon it by the collapse of Mughal central authority.*

Left: *The Governor of Bombay with district officials in 1943. He is flanked by the British collector or head of the district and the Indian superintendent of police. Behind them stand the local revenue officers, whose ranks remained entirely Indian throughout the Raj.*

Right: *The Madras High Court.*
British Indian high courts,
established in the 1860s,
imposed British legal principles
and procedures on India's
varied customary law.
Below: *Indian judicial and*
executive officers with British
seniors in a Punjab district.
Indians were excluded from the
élite ICS and from the higher
ranks of the police and
judiciary until political reforms
opened the doors to
Indianisation in the 1920s.
Below right: *'Our Judge', a*
nineteenth-century lithograph
of a district court. Although
British judges, assisted by
Indian subordinates, usually
showed a sound grasp of local
customs, court proceedings had
their funnier moments.

Right: *Sepoys of the Madras Army, the first Indian force raised by the East India Company in 1748. It was Indian troops who enabled British traders to conquer a sub-continent.*
Below: *Indian sepoys in action in Gujerat, 1849. Their mutiny eight years later marked the final bid by feudal India to overthrow British rule.*

Left: *Lieutenant Prem Bhagat of the Royal Bombay Sappers & Miners, the first Indian to win the Victoria Cross during the Second World War, retired as a general in independent India. Few Indians were accepted into the officer corps of the British Indian army until the war forced the pace of Indianisation.*
Below: *Ratings of the Royal Indian Navy, which expanded rapidly during the war. Their anti-British feeling resulted in the Mutiny of 1946, which dealt the Raj its final blow.*

Top: *The Tata steelworks at Jamshedpur, founded by Indian business despite British scepticism.*
Left: *J. N. Tata (1839–1904), founding father of India's leading industrial empire.*
Above: *Tata's Bombay mansion, one of the earliest and grandest examples of a westernised Indian home.*
Above right: *Bombay traders bidding for British goods, 1836.*
Right: *Eighteenth-century miniature of an Indian prince entertaining British officers. Under the Raj, the sahibs mixed far less freely with Indians.*

Top: *The Royal Bombay Yacht Club, which barred Indians from entering, even if they happened to be Maharajas.*
Above: *The Bengal Club, Calcutta, which restricted entry to 'respectable European bachelors only'. Its fine building had to be sold after independence to meet financial losses.*

everyone was on tenterhooks while the white man was there; and you could see that they were suffering as much as we were. There was no really human contact between the white and the black.

Social mixing under the Raj, enmeshed both in British class and racial prejudices and in Indian caste and sexual taboos, could never be entirely relaxed. But there were always outstanding individuals, British and Indian, who broke through the barriers. Tara Ali Baig offers the example of a British district officer who stayed on after independence.

He was a very unusual British officer, because I think he was the only one I ever met who spoke perfect Bengali. He was very looked down upon by his clan as a consequence, because it wasn't done to go native. He was a man of exceptional intellect, and the Indians in the whole district had a tremendously high regard for him. . . . In fact, he was threatened at times with severe censure for his fraternising with them, particularly for going into people's homes and sitting in some of the traditional houses in the kitchen of a traditional Bengali woman and chatting with her. She thought this was enchanting, because they had never found an Englishman who was so friendly.

Indian women, as a rule, had far less contact with the sahibs than their husbands; but there were exceptions. By the 1930s, the Indian upper classes could boast some formidable women, products of Western emancipation, who were far more at home on committees, dance-floors and tennis-courts than in the seclusion of the traditional Indian *zenana* (women's quarters). One of this new generation of Indian women, Tara Ali Baig, describes her first encounter with an unconventional British governor, Lord Brabourne.

He was a very dashing young man in those days. I believe he had some Spanish ancestry. And he certainly was not going to toe the line of the manner in which British governors had functioned previous to that. In those days, Government House in Bombay always had a dinner and a ball after that. It was considered a great thing to be invited. The very senior people were invited to dinner. The junior people were invited to the ball; and being very junior at the time, we were invited to the ball. The very first dance, Brabourne came up and asked me to dance. The very senior baronets' wives, the Parsi[1] dowagers, they were all there in their diamonds; and they were absolutely scandalised that the Governor should not have someone brought up to him to dance, but that he should go across to talk to somebody who was completely unknown, and certainly not in their social register, to have the first dance. It was considered very scandalous.

1 The Parsis, one of India's smallest minorities, are a community of ancient Persian extraction. They were among the first Indians to westernise, led the commercial and other professions and tended to be ardently pro-British. Many were rewarded for their loyalty with knighthoods and baronetcies.

Such behaviour became less scandalous in the twilight of the Raj during the Second World War. This had a lot to do with the arrival in India of thousands of young British servicemen, many of whom had not had time to acquire the traditional prejudices of the old colonials. Their presence changed the ethos, not only within the armed forces, but in civilian life too, as Khushwant Singh describes.

Many of them were young Communists or socialists, and they were appalled. They wouldn't join these whites-only clubs, and they wanted to be invited to Indian homes. I remember some of them coming and staying with us, on the slightest pretext wanting to cultivate Indians. That made a lot of difference, because a lot of the bitterness in the Indians' mind was taken away by the presence of these people, because they were keener to make friends with Indians than mix with their own lot. . . . Not many Indian women were advanced enough to be able to mix with them; but some did, the type which went ballroom dancing. And there were many affairs between them; some even got married to white people at the time, which was unknown before.

In tune with the changing times, a new social scene sprang up outside the stuffy clubs of the old Anglo-India. Raj Chatterji remembers New Delhi, the imperial capital which sprang up during the Twenties and Thirties, as the setting for a more relaxed and cosmopolitan night-life, in which ballroom dancing helped break the social ice between the British and Indians.

You had these tea-rooms, like Wenger's and Davico's, which were very popular. They had tea-dances, and you could get a very good meal there. There was this famous place, the Astoria Ballroom, where you had a tea-dance on Wednesdays and a Saturday night dance as the normal run. . . . Mostly, you'd find in those early days, the British side were civilians working in the Government of India – you know, joint secretaries, deputy secretaries. And of course, during the war, plenty of army people, until the day when places like the Astoria were completely taken over by the Yanks. By that time, there were many Indian ICS men whose wives danced, smoked, drank the odd sherry. They were there, so there was mixed dancing. Normally, you'd see separate tables. I'd say it wasn't really until the war that things opened up and you could see mixed parties.

Unfortunately, the social relaxation of the 1940s came far too late to heal racial scars that were a century old. And even then, the liberalism of British newcomers was scant compensation for the continuing arrogance of the die-hards. Incidents of racial humiliation were an everyday occurrence for most Indians who encountered the British; and even upper-crust loyalists did not escape. The most visible symbols of white supremacy were the 'Europeans Only' compartments in first-class railway carriages. And even where there was no official colour-bar,

British travellers often claimed a right to monopolise railway compartments. Rajeshwar Dayal, an ICS officer who was then Home Secretary of the United Provinces, remembers such an occasion when his wife was travelling.

> My wife was taking the train from Kanpur to come to Lucknow. Her father was a member of the Viceroy's Executive Council and a leading industrialist of Kanpur, an extremely well-known family. She began to enter the first-class compartment at Kanpur station. She was escorted by a number of people – her father's secretaries and station staff. But she was refused entry by a British officer, sitting there with a couple of Alsatian dogs, who told her she couldn't enter. She said: 'Why not?' He said: 'If you try to enter, I'll let my dogs loose on you.' She was taken aback and said: 'How dare you!' He said: 'Well, you try.' She called him some names, referred to his ill-manners and said the train would not go without her in that compartment. The station staff begged her not to insist; they'd add another bogey to the train; but she insisted. Finally, she did get in, she had her way. There was no conversation between them during the journey of an hour and a half; but he apparently learned subsequently who she was. And he turned out to be a colonel or a brigadier who was serving in Delhi in the same department of which my father-in-law was the head in the Viceroy's Cabinet. And he had the temerity later on to complain against her to my father-in-law and say: 'Your daughter was very rude to me. She called me a gutter-snipe.' This kind of incident in 1946, one year before independence!

The Raj never legislated an official colour-bar. But whether on the railways, or in the shops and streets, Indians were expected to know their place. According to Sankara Menon, a South Indian theosophist and educationist, the discrimination Indians experienced may often have been trivial, but it was nonetheless galling, because it was so pervasive.

> There was no apartheid, but still they got preference in all sorts of things. We were only second-class citizens. If we went to Spencer's [the biggest department store in Madras], there'd be some third-rate Englishman waiting to buy something. I would have gone there long ahead of him, but I would have to wait to be served till that fellow was served. In everything it was like that. There was nothing which it did not touch and soil.

Even the world of sport was not free of racial segregation and tension. Both football and cricket had become immensely popular with Indians by the 1920s; and Indian teams were often good enough to beat the British at their own games. British service teams were not averse to playing Indians, largely because of the shortage of rival British teams whom they could play. But the mixed matches which might have brought the races closer together rarely produced any genuine camaraderie between players or spectators. According to M. S. Ramaswamy, the oldest surviving sports commentator of the *Indian Express* newspaper in Madras, Indian teams were not allowed to use the same pavilions or facilities as their British opponents, and even the glasses out of which they drank were sterilised before being used again.

In this sort of atmosphere, it was hardly surprising that the game itself developed into a test of colonial versus nationalist loyalties. Jatin Chakrabarti, a former boxing champion and later a leading patron of Indian football, remembers how the Mohun Bagan Football Club in Calcutta was a symbol of nationalist victory for him and many other young supporters because it had defeated a British team and won the Indian Football Association Shield in 1911. He maintains that there would have been many more such triumphs for Indian sport if British referees had been less racially biased.

> I do remember that in 1924 or '26, in the final of the Indian Football Association Shield, there was heavy rain. In that rain, the ground was practically flooded, and it was very muddy and slushy. The game ought to have been stopped; but as the Indians were playing barefooted, without any boots, it was to their greatest disadvantage; and the referee gave the opinion that the ground was quite fit for game. The Mohun Bagan team was defeated by three or four goals to nil. On a muddy, slushy ground, it is quite obvious that sometimes when you try to block a player within the penalty area, you may fall on the ground, or your opponent may fall on the ground. On that particular occasion, taking into consideration the condition of the ground, the penalty kick ought not to have been awarded. But it was awarded by that notorious referee who is still remembered by us. Whenever he used to be a referee in any game, everybody took it for granted that whenever he gets any opportunity he will give his award against the Indians.

Such feelings of discrimination made every Indian, however non-political, a potential nationalist. The racial exclusiveness and prejudice of Anglo-Indian society was not confined to social contact with Indians. Culturally, it took the form of an overwhelming rejection of and contempt for India's traditional learning and arts, with a corresponding emphasis on the superiority of Western values and education. And yet, paradoxically, this very emphasis on westernisation was to foster a cultural challenge to colonial rule from Indians schooled, not only in ballroom dancing, but in Western notions of individual freedom and dissent.

AT ARM'S LENGTH
EXCHANGING CULTURES

*Gandhi himself, Tagore and theosophists like Mrs Besant were
able to convey to the world the whole range of Indian thought
and philosophy only through English. But for the English
language, the best things in India could not have been known to
the rest of the world. It was a medium of commerce in philosophy
and poetry. . . . You receive an influence either directly or
indirectly as a provocation. English provided the dialectical
opposite which made India look into herself and find wonderful
things within herself.*

K. *Swaminathan (former Professor of English, Madras University)*

As with the peoples of India, so with their languages, religions and
culture, the British went through distinct phases of exploration,
assimilation and rejection. Founders of the empire, like Warren
Hastings, the first British Governor-General, had a healthy respect for
and curiosity about a civilisation far more ancient than their own, even
if it was alien to Christian ethics and Western rationalism. The first
generation of British administrators studied Indian languages and
religious classics and took over the role of the Mughals as patrons of art
and learning. The East India Company made financial grants to
traditional educational establishments and endowed various new
societies and institutes for Oriental or 'Asiatic' studies.

By the middle of the nineteenth century, such curiosity and eclecticism had been replaced by a new, crusading imperialism. Its main
elements were an ideological justification of empire as a civilising
mission, and a commitment to reorganising Indian society on the basis
of Western moral, legal and educational values. The positive side of this
new definition of empire was increasing state intervention to promote
social reforms, such as the abolition of *sati*[1] and child marriage and the
lifting of the ban on the remarriage of widows. But along with such
benefits went the notion of the White Man's Burden and the denigration
of Indians as racially inferior and culturally backward. Imperial
contempt for India's indigenous heritage persisted till independence,
and its memory still rankles with Indian scholars like Sankara Menon,
who is President of the Madras theosophists' educational centre at
Kalakshetra.

The British were a very blind people. . . . Except in the case of a
very few people who were deep students, they did not make any
attempt during their 250 years here in this country to contact

1 The Hindu religious practice of self-immolation by widows.

Indian thinking. They wouldn't know what the *Bhagavad Gita*[1]
contained, what the *Upanishads*[2] contained, what the *Zend
Avesta*[3] contained. They did not know any Indian art, in spite of
the great art that there is. Today everybody comes from the West to
hear our music and see our dancing; but in those days, no
Englishman would come to see any of these things, absolutely not.
They thought that it was *infra dig* to do so, that they would lose
caste if they did. And so these things languished for want of
patronage, except in the Indian [princely] states.

The new imperialism brought with it the proselytising work of
Christian missionaries; and neglect of Indian art became a virtue in their
campaign to win Indian converts. Malcolm Adiseshiah, an eminent
academic and former Vice-Chancellor of Madras University, is the son of
a first-generation Anglican convert from Hinduism. While he remains
loyal to his Christian upbringing, he concedes that the missionaries'
attitude to Indian art was coloured, not only by religious prejudice, but
by a strong dose of Victorian prudery.

On idol-worship in the Hindu temples, they were most critical. And
then they were also most critical of the Hindu, south Indian dance,
Bharata Natyam, which in those days was only practised by the
devadasis, the prostitutes of the temple. They were prostitutes to
God, not prostitutes to men. But the missionaries were most critical
of these aspects of Indian culture and asked us Christians to keep
out of that. . . . They felt that all the sculptures in the temples were
vulgar, not art forms. It's only today that we've begun to see that
these are expressions of art. But they regarded this as a demeaning
and corrupting influence.

First in the field were the Catholic missions, fanning out from their
original base in the Portuguese colony of Goa on the west coast. Anglican
and other Protestant denominations followed; but as Adiseshiah
explains, they placed less emphasis on winning mass conversions.

The Catholics were more successful in making converts because
they went in for a much larger programme of subsidising the poor.
They deliberately went around working among the scheduled
[lower] castes, scheduled [backward] tribes, fishermen and very
backward people, whereas the Anglican Church worked among the
Brahmins, the topmost in society. So part of the Anglican effort is
to be seen in the quality of people who came into their fold. . . . The
Anglicans that I knew were much more concerned with trying to
help the poor rise above their poverty by training them in skills, by
opening vocational institutions, rather than converting them. The
Catholics went all out first to convert them, and then would give
them the bowl of rice. The Anglicans played the thing according to

1 A philosophical poem regarded as the central sacred text of Hinduism.
2 Ancient Hindu religious commentaries composed from 700 BC onwards.
3 The Zoroastrian scriptures of India's Parsi community, migrants from pre-Islamic Iran.

the rules of Christianity, which is to help people in whatever condition they are, before you try to convert them.

Most Indian converts to Christianity were therefore Catholics recruited from the caste and tribal groups whom orthodox Hinduism had traditionally oppressed and exploited. But there were exceptions, like Adiseshiah's father, a Brahmin whose family took legal action to avert the shame of his conversion.

> My father was the only member of a family of about 26 people who became a Christian. When he was in school, listening to the Bible exposition every day in class, he came to realise that the God that was being expounded by Jesus Christ and the Gospels was far more real to him than the gods of the Hindu pantheon that came to him through his father. Being a Brahmin, he and his brothers used to repeat all the Hindu scriptures by heart every day; and so he was able to compare one with the other. This led him to go to the head of the institution one day and say: 'I wish to become a Christian.' My father's parents were furious, and they took him to court. When the Magistrate asked him: 'Why have you become a Christian?' he quoted a verse from the Bible: 'There is no other God on earth except Jesus Christ.'

Incidents like this were the nightmare of every orthodox Hindu or Muslim parent whose children attended a mission school. Yet, for the vast majority, the impact of Christianity proved cultural rather than religious. Both Hinduism and Islam were religions too ancient and deeply entrenched to be swept aside by a Christian tide; nor was this ever an aim of British rule. The Raj and its officials were, from the outset, a secular authority that practised a policy of benevolent neutrality towards and between the various Christian missions. The missionaries made themselves invaluable to government by providing in the voluntary sector the English-medium schools which the official policy of Western education required; and they received government grants for this purpose. But the alliance between colonial church and state stopped well short of any direct interference with India's traditional beliefs, especially after the religious backlash which had fuelled the Mutiny of 1857.

When the British left in 1947, India's Christian population numbered a mere 7.4 million in a country of 400 millions. Yet a far larger proportion of Indians had undergone, in some respects, a more profound conversion. They had become westernised, or at any rate anglicised. There were, of course, degrees of anglicisation; and a mastery of the English language and its literature did not necessarily imply a slavish imitation of Western ways. In southern India, especially, with its long and unbroken tradition of Hindu scholarship, the Western-educated intelligentsia remained strongly rooted in traditional ways. As M. S. Ramaswamy, a veteran Madras journalist, remarks, few south Indians adopted Western clothes.

> There were a few anglicised Indians who used to wear a *topee* [hat] and a tie and waistcoat and all those things. . . . Those who wanted

to curry favour with the British would dress this way, but not the average man. Most of the lawyers did not wear trousers; they wore *dhotis*[1] and a big handsome turban.

Professor K. Swaminathan, who has spent most of his eighty years teaching English literature at Madras University, describes his contemporaries as 'Indians who had learned English, rather than uprooted Englishmen'. 'People in Bengal,' he says, 'became anglicised sooner and more completely than people in Madras, largely because in Madras there was always a tradition of Sanskrit and Tamil combined. The rootedness of the south Indian in his own past arises from the fact that the period of Muslim domination was shorter here than in the north.'

The north, with its tradition of assimilating so many waves of foreign invasion and settlement, was far more extreme in its westernisation, whether in dress, social manners or domestic habits. The result was often an absurd and awkward imitation of the British. Khushwant Singh, whose family come from a modest, peasant background in Punjab, describes the changes that upward mobility brought when his father became a successful builder in Delhi.

We had sofas and that kind of thing. We sat in chairs, like the English did, not on *charpais*;[2] and we had carpets. My father, being a little anglicised, was able to go abroad and came back with fancy notions. For instance, on every state occasion, he wore striped trousers and spats with his turban and tie and tried to imitate the English as much as he could being a Sikh. But otherwise, our food was entirely Indian, except when we invited an Englishman. . . . My father tried to get my mother to learn English. He even hired an 'Anglo-Indian' lady to teach her; but she proved completely unteachable. She just couldn't cope with the language; and apart from saying 'Thank you,' and 'Good Morning,' or 'Good Evening', her vocabulary never went beyond that. My father taught himself with great pain, and was able to converse quite easily with English people with his own Punjabi accent.

According to Khushwant Singh, the most obvious contrast between traditional and Western life-styles was in the drab, whitewashed uniformity of the colonial bungalows into which Indians of the aspiring middle class moved.

The traditional Indian home of the well-to-do was always built round a courtyard. The Muslim home would have separate apartments for ladies, and the visitor was stopped at the *deori*, where the men met each other. With the British, it was quite different. The bungalow was the British concept. It always had a garden around it, and it was open on all sides, and the servants' quarters were removed away from it. With the Indian home, the

1 The *dhoti* is an untailored length of cloth wound around the waist and legs.
2 A *charpai* is a settee made of rope.

servants lived in the same premises in a corner. So these were the basic differences in the architecture. The well-to-do Indian home had in the courtyard a pigeon-loft, almost inevitably a small jasmine-garden, where the women could take their walks, and frequently a fountain or two. If it was a Muslim home, it would have a mosque inside the house; and if it was a Hindu home, it would have its own temple. None of these were there in the British homes.

It was a period when being westernised meant being 'advanced'; and social life in the westernised Indian home followed British fashions as closely as possible. Tara Ali Baig says that her parents' home in Dacca became a sort of Indian substitute for the local European club.

In those days, the club, which had the tennis-courts and so on, was banned to us Indians. So our house became a sort of alternative club, and many people would drop in for tennis in the afternoon. . . . There were quite a lot of young officials; there were young army people as well. My parents, being very modern, had no concept of segregating us for the sake of marriage. So it was just enjoyment, a dinner-party followed by dancing. We had the wind-up gramophones at that time; none of the sophisticated, technical stuff that you have now. A lot of our young people were educated in England; and they would come back, as they do today, with lots of records.

Because there was no such thing as TV, we invented lots of entertainments. One of them was a thing called a 'Progressive Party'. You would have soup at one person's house, and then the whole crowd would go on to the next person's house and have fish, and the next course at the next house, and so on. And then there were games in which you were partnered, and you went off in any vehicle which happened to be there and had to collect certain things and bring them back by a certain time to win the prizes. One of the items I can remember was a *tonga*[1] and horse; and suddenly there was this clatter of horses and *tongas* coming in the front drive, because people had been very successful in being able to collect that item at least!

More significant than Western party games was the gradual emergence of Indian women from their centuries-old segregation into mixed company. Contrary to Western assumptions, life in the traditional *zenana* or harem had not necessarily meant ignorance or backwardness, as Tara Ali Baig reminds us.

There was a tremendous amount of sophistication even in traditional families. Within even an orthodox Hindu family, the amount of learning that a woman might have was far greater than people recognised. She may not have gone to school, but she was

---

1 A two-wheeled carriage.

taught at home, and there was a great deal of learning in our old scriptures. It was the same with Muslim women. . . . It was a woman's world. It's not as though they were kept in a kind of prison or withheld from everything in the world.

Even so, Western influences produced a new generation of Indian women, some of whom were as much at home with the traditional accomplishments of the *zenana* as they were in a Western ballroom. By the 1930s, it was becoming increasingly fashionable for the daughters of some of India's leading families to attend English-medium schools and universities, often abroad, and to acquire social graces like tennis and ballroom dancing. Even some of the more orthodox Muslim households, where *purdah* or the veil survived, allowed a good deal of latitude behind the veil. Tara Ali Baig describes how her father and she became agents of change in the Nawab of Dacca's *zenana*.

The Nawab's family being Muslim, the women were in *purdah*. . . . But they were educated; and when they went to the hills in the summer months, they would even go riding. One day, Mother had a *purdah* tea-party for the ladies of the Nawab's house. They came out of their car in a sort of funnel of cloth, to protect them from the gaze of anybody who might be inadvertently standing around, and came inside. And then everything was ruined, because my father walked in the door. He was a very sociable fellow, and he saw that they were not in the least upset by his presence. So he sat down and started talking to them. And that's how *purdah* was virtually broken in Dacca at the time.

But they also wanted the enjoyments of Western life, and one of them was swimming. They asked me whether I would teach them to swim. In all the big houses in Bengal, there were these water-tanks with steps going down into them. When they asked me what they should wear – they were thinking of wearing saris – I said: 'Nothing doing! I'm not going to have to rescue all of you with this wet cloth round your necks. You have got to wear bathing-suits.' There were screams of horror – that their legs and arms would be exposed. I said: 'Yes, but nobody's going to see you, so why worry?' Eventually, they got into bathing-suits, and I did teach them some swimming. It wasn't the world's greatest Olympic event, but it was great fun.

Westernisation, of course, was not just a matter of social manners. It included language, ideas and values; and in these areas the colonial period, paradoxically, proved one of the most creative in India's intellectual history.

With the exception of the few British who 'went native', cultural exchange between India and its colonial rulers was a predominantly one-way traffic. Yet the colonial challenge produced its own antithesis by stimulating a cultural renaissance, out of which grew a new political nationalism. The pioneer of this renaissance was Raja Ram Mohan Roy, the nineteenth-century Bengali intellectual and reformer, whose work helped bridge the divide between Mughal India and the Raj. He founded the Brahmo Samaj movement, which was essentially an attempt to meet the challenge of Christianity by incorporating much of its ethics into a reformed Hinduism. Brahmo Samajists, based in Bengal, aimed at purifying Hindu society by a return to the philosophical basis of the ancient Hindu scriptures, rejecting the idolatry and superstition of later generations, and with them social evils like caste prejudice and the suppression of women.

By the end of the nineteenth century, the Bengali renaissance had found an outstanding exponent in Rabindranath Tagore, who carried its art and ideas to the rest of India and abroad. Equally at home in Eastern and Western cultures, Tagore symbolised the eclectic and enquiring spirit of a new Indian intelligentsia which could borrow freely from the West without being swallowed by it. Knighted by the Raj, and awarded the Nobel Prize for Literature, Tagore became India's cultural ambassador abroad, fêted and celebrated around the world, whether in New York or Tokyo. But he remained a committed nationalist throughout the long half-century that he reigned as India's philosopher-king. His cultural roots lay firmly in Bengal, where his *ashram*, Santiniketan, was the home of a new school of Indian art, Romantic Revivalism, and of ambitious educational experiments. Renuka Ray, a frequent visitor to the *ashram*, says that his influence extended far beyond philosophy.

The entire Tagore family had a great deal to do with the revival of culture, not only in Bengal but throughout India. Even before Rabindranath's time, the wife of his eldest brother, Satyendranath Tagore, who was in the ICS, had a great deal to do with the revival of Indian dress. For instance, the sari, the way we wear it now, going about and making it more usable than the way that *purdah* women would use it, was started first by her. . . . They wanted to bring back the best in the old, in line with modern ideas and conditions. . . . Rabindranath Tagore was the first to go east and rebuild our bridges with other Eastern countries; because there had been a complete break, during British colonisation, between all the countries of the East. Ram Mohan Roy had suggested it; but Tagore was the first to go to all these countries – Indonesia, Malaya, Japan and China – and bring back things from there.

As Renuka Ray points out, Tagore's sense of Eastern solidarity did not mean a rejection of British and European culture: 'He was a very fine writer in Bengali; but he said: "Languages grow and take words from other languages, and there's no harm in it. English is a very beautiful language, and there's no reason why we should not take words from that language." '

One of Tagore's most passionate concerns was to provide an Indian alternative to what he regarded as the strait-jacket of the Anglo-Indian education offered by the mission schools.

At Santiniketan, his idea was of an international university, giving schooling of the type he thought was right. Children should have natural surroundings; in fact, the school was held in the gardens mostly. He didn't like children being forced into routine ways. . . . He brought back some of the conceptions of the schools of the old *rishis* [sages] of India, where the children were taught outside activities and their artistic side was developed. He wanted an all-round education and not only book-learning.

A similar cultural revival in the south, which also attempted to synthesise East and West, was led by the Madras Theosophical Society. Its presiding deity was Dr Annie Besant, an Irish Home-Rule campaigner who settled in India at the turn of the century and became the grand old lady of the Indian nationalist movement. Her followers were a curious mixture of mystics, vegetarians, aesthetes and political activists. But they were united by a search for common ground between Indian and European religious and cultural traditions. Sankara Menon, a veteran theosophist, explains the importance of the movement.

The Theosophical Society under Annie Besant brought into India a large number of Westerners who were India-oriented. She herself said that she was not Western but Indian. She encouraged Indian life and thought, Indian forms of art. . . . Before Gandhi, she was the greatest encourager of national culture, the national spirit. She established schools and colleges all over India, where the emphasis was on patriotism, living the simple Indian life, cultivating Indian values.

Theosophy had strong links with Indian nationalism, not least because theosophists like Annie Besant played a prominent role in the moderate wing of the Indian National Congress. Like Tagore at Santiniketan, Mrs Besant presided over an educational centre in Madras where she experimented with her spiritual and nationalist ideas. But as M. S. Ramaswamy explains, the appeal of theosophy to most Indians was secular rather than religious.

The Theosophical Society brought us some foreigners who said that Indian religion and culture were not something to be ashamed of, were something to be proud of. That was why many Indians welcomed them. Though theosophy is supposed to be a synthetic religion, it pays considerable attention to Hinduism. Those were days when everything Hindu was looked down upon; but these gentlemen gave us courage and encouragement. That's why you find a very large number of Indians were members of the Society, without really accepting all that theosophy taught. They picked out the Hindu part of it and let go the rest.

The Madras theosophists and the Bengali revivalists were part of an East-West dialogue that rejected colonial values and education, while assimilating what was positive in Christian and European thought. As

Professor Swaminathan of Madras reminds us, the English language in India was more than an administrative convenience. It brought European literature, through English translations, within reach of educated Indians and enabled India to export her own classics to the rest of the world.

For many years, English replaced the local languages and Sanskrit. But in course of time, largely because of the influence of European Indologists and educational psychologists, the Indian languages got a fillip through English. English was a powerful influence on the creative literature in those languages. Many Sanskrit works were made popular through English renderings of them or English commentaries on them. Gandhi, for example, read the *Gita* for the first time in Edwin Arnold's translation. People like Aurobindo,[1] Vivekananda,[2] Mahatma Gandhi, were able to control, influence so many Indians because they knew the English language, and it was through English that they could talk to the rest of India.

After the conquest of India by the West, the reaction has been the conquest of the rest of the world by India. In 1893, things happened which made it impossible for the modern world to ignore and neglect *Vedanta*:[3] Mahatma Gandhi went to South Africa; Vivekananda went to America; Sri Aurobindo came back to India after years in England; Mrs Annie Besant came to India. All these things amounted to a spiritual and intellectual conquest of the West by Indian thought.

While English translations of Indian classics enabled people in different parts of the sub-continent to rediscover and explore a common heritage, the process also operated in reverse. The translation into vernacular languages of the Bible and other Christian literature helped to revive and strengthen several Indian languages, as Swaminathan explains.

The missionaries' motive was not to encourage these languages, but to make them serve their purpose. But they did a good job; they produced dictionaries, grammars and good translations. The translation of the Bible into various Indian languages was itself a great contribution to the development of these languages.

According to Swaminathan, the colonial conquest triggered a dialectical interaction between East and West, in classrooms and academies across the land, which, far from suppressing Indian culture, acted in the long term as a stimulant to rediscovery and revival.

For many Indians, it was a challenge which they took up and reacted to by recognising the immense superiority of their own

1 Aurobindo Ghosh (1872–1950) started his career as a revolutionary nationalist, inspired by Hindu revivalism, but retired from politics in 1910 to found a religious *ashram* named after him at Auroville in the French enclave of Pondicherry.
2 Swami Vivekananda (1863–1902), one of the most important leaders of the Hindu religious revival during the nineteenth century, who related traditional Hinduism to Western ideas of social service and national self-reliance.
3 The mystical philosophy of the ancient Hindu scriptures, the *Vedas*.

heritage. I can give hundreds of examples of people who started with British criticism of something Indian, and then studied the thing Indian and found that the British had misunderstood and underestimated its value . . . the *Ramayana*[1], for example. In the beginning, they ran down the *Ramayana*. When the criticism was taken seriously and people went back to the ancient, traditional sources, they found that the *Ramayana* looks childish to begin with, but that it is also an excellent book for grown-ups, because it is not so much a drama as an allegory. So every challenge from Christian or Western critics has resulted in a rediscovery of the real worth of the Indian traditional heritage.

The negative point is the feeling of inferiority that they gave us. But then we did not succumb to it. We rebelled against it in a positive way; and we tried to make up for it by rediscovering our own past and by doing, in a better way, what the British did.

The instrument of this cultural rebellion was, ironically, the very language which the Raj had introduced for its own convenience; and English was to become a double-edged sword in the hands of Indian nationalists.

1 The most popular Hindu religious epic, which tells the story of King Rama, regarded as an incarnation of the god Vishnu.

CHILDREN OF EMPIRE

Prima in Indis, Gateway of India,
Door of the East with its face to the West,
Here in Bombay we are living and learning
India, our country, to give you our best.

Cathedral School song

Founded in 1860 as the choir-school of the Anglican diocese of Bombay, the Cathedral School was one of the earliest and most exclusive of thousands of English-medium high schools set up under the Raj. Some were established by the state, a few by Maharajas and other Indian benefactors, and many more by the various Christian missions. Regardless of religious denomination, they remain clubbed together in the Indian mind as 'convent schools'. Most of them began with the aim of looking after the education of Christians, either Indian converts, or 'Anglo-Indians' (Eurasians of mixed descent), or the sprinkling of British families who could not afford to send their children back to school in Britain. Till the end of the Raj, the convent schools were dominated by these groups; but from the turn of the century onwards, they had to open their doors to non-Christian Indians as a condition of government grant-aid. Although rituals like morning assembly and religious teaching remained firmly Christian, the mission schools became less concerned with winning religious converts than with fostering a new class of anglicised Indians, through whom the values of the Raj might filter down to the rest of the Indian people. The values they prized were those of the British public schools – honesty, discipline and team-spirit – as Malcolm Adiseshiah, a prominent Indian Christian educationist, recalls.

One very important value was honesty, because the Hindu tradition doesn't pay much attention to being absolutely honest. One of the curious things my mother used to say was: 'Tell the truth like an Englishman.' And it was true, that we never said 'No'. In Tamil, my language, if you say 'No', it's bad manners. So even though you mean 'No', you'll say 'Yes'. Now this kind of thing, we learnt, is out. It was one of the things that the Christian institutions taught us; and Gandhiji came later on and picked it up and made it the essential of his system.

The second thing they taught us was service. . . . There wasn't a tradition of religion serving the people, whether in education or in health. It was a completely new approach that the Christian missionaries brought in using their religious motivation to open up schools and colleges, hospitals and clinics.

Along with Christian ethics went an often incongruous imitation of the secular ceremonial of the great British public schools – neo-Gothic cloisters and quadrangles, prefects and monitors clad in ties and blazers, and fish fingers and jam roll for dinner. Even a day school like the Cathedral was divided up into 'Houses', each with its own colours, to encourage the competitive team-spirit at games and exams; and its school song was set to the music of Harrow's 'Forty Years On'. Like their British models, the schools of the Raj laid great store by patriotism. But the patriotism they celebrated was British; and for Indians under British rule that could be confusing. Harindranath Chattopadhyaya, the veteran nationalist poet, went to school in the early years of the century and remembers growing up with considerable reverence for Queen Victoria and the Empire.

> My mother used to talk about Queen Victoria as the mother of the country. I remember her sixteen servants used to sit around her every evening in the courtyard, and she used to talk about Queen Victoria and praise her and say she is doing so much for the poor. . . . I remember, when I was in school, every day we were made to sing 'Britannia Rule the Waves, Britons never, never, never shall be slaves'. Now I loved the word 'waves'. The poetic side of me accepted the word 'waves'; and, of course, along with the waves, I accepted the whole song. I didn't know what I was singing until it was pointed out to me later by my father: 'Baby, you know, you mustn't sing that song, it's not necessary. You're trying to say that Britons will never be slaves, but why should anyone be a slave?' So I ceased to sing that song. Instead I sang 'Home, Sweet Home'!

In the prime of their civilising mission, colonial educationists often acted as though education itself was a colonial gift to India. Lord Macaulay, the British administrator who pioneered the introduction of Western education, is best remembered by Indians today as an arrogant, if well-meaning, westerniser who believed that 'everything in classical Sanskrit could be put into half a shelf of a Western library.' His predecessors had been well aware that the learning of the East was every bit as voluminous and far more ancient than the scholarship of the West. The problem with their policy of funding traditional centres of education was that the Raj increasingly needed a disciplined, English-speaking cadre of Indians, first as clerks and commercial agents and later in more senior positions in its judicial and revenue administration. The traditional system of education, preoccupied with classical literature and religious law and metaphysics, could not be easily adapted to such utilitarian ends. Language, too, was a major obstacle, since traditional learning, whether Hindu or Muslim, required a knowledge of classical languages like Sanskrit, Arabic or Persian (the Mughal court language) and was therefore a virtual monopoly of the priestly and upper castes.

There were obvious parallels with the dominance of Latin in medieval Europe; but in India the reformation was imposed by colonial fiat and its instrument was not the vernacular languages but English. Macaulay's famous Minute of 1835 made English-medium education on Western lines the official aim of British policy in India. Since the British rulers had no intention of subsidising major public expenditure on mass education, implementation was gradual and selective, left largely to the private enterprise of Christian missions and later of Indian philanthropists who chose to emulate them. The Government switched its grant-aid from traditional Hindu and Muslim academies to English-medium higher education. Inevitably, the new learning, like the old, remained largely the preserve of upper-caste Indians, based mainly in the urban centres, who were already educated and affluent enough to take advantage of it. Primary education, especially in rural areas, lagged far behind, a problem which continues to bedevil India's development, according to the economist Ashok Mitra.

> The major indictment that I would make against the British was the fact that they completely turned away from their duty and obligation to educate the people – the neglect of elementary and primary education, which is the key issue in any type of development, economic as well as social. If only they had neglected everything else, forgotten about railway development, textiles, extraction from the mines, and concentrated on elementary education, this would be a different country today. What they did, they did for their own selfish cause; and there is no question that they set this nation back by at least a hundred years, if not more. . . . They should have set up primary schools all over the country, blanketed the villages and towns with primary schools, so that instead of a rate of literacy in 1947 which was hovering around 25 per cent, it could have been at least 75 or 80 per cent.

Colonial education, as preached by Macaulay and practised by the Christian missions, may have neglected the rural masses and denied India's indigenous cultural heritage; but it also created its own nemesis in the shape of a new class of westernised Indians who quickly outgrew the clerical role for which they were reared. British teachers played their part in this process. Not all of them were missionaries or colonialists, and some were outstanding educators. Romesh Thapar, one of India's leading political journalists, remembers how, as a drop-out from boarding school, he was rescued by a dedicated British headmaster in Lahore.

> I came out of Bishop Cotton School, which was a kind of Anglo-India. I'd been dumped there for eight years by my father, who was in the military. There was no way he could organise my education, except by putting me into a boarding school of that sort. Of course, the collaborating élite in those days looked up to boarding schools as *the* thing, because there were boarding schools in England, and the best went to them.
> When I came out of boarding school, I had failed my Senior Cambridge. I was a gawky sort of sixteen, and I spoke a kind of Indian Welsh. My father looked at me and said: 'What the hell am I

going to do with you?' He said: 'I've discovered that there's a man called Barrie who's taken over the Aitchison Chief's College. He wants commoners from good families, to train them up and show his Council that they should broaden the base of the school.' So I was flung into Aitchison Chief's College, which was the centre of education for all the feudal nobility of north India. They all had their suites of rooms and servants and horses, etc. I was the first commoner. They used to call me 'Bloody Tommy' – until I was put into the boxing-ring with them and played hell into them, because I was trained in that from Bishop Cotton. Then they started being more respectful.

Barrie took so much interest in me, in order to prove his experiment, that I was transformed within six months. I was a serious student; I was reading in the library regularly, literally a book a day almost; I was studying Persian under a wonderful man who taught me so fast that I translated *The Deerslayer* by Fenimore Cooper into Modern Persian, and it became a textbook when I was eighteen.

Barrie used to take me out in his garden and walk me through the trees and say: 'Now, address a meeting! I want to change your way of speaking. I want to give you new emphasis. You must speak without an accent – you're an Indian.' He changed my speech, he changed my breathing when I was speaking; he made me sing all kinds of songs to the trees. I became totally hooked on the man; and I suddenly realised that I had a father. He then began to teach me that I was an Indian, and that meant that I should not take all the rubbish that I read in the newspapers as gospel, that I must learn about my country, my people, their traumas, their poverty. He began to give me a kind of *New Statesman* education. And gradually, he moved me into giving General Knowledge lectures to my fellow-students.

When my father, after two years, talked with him, he said he was very grateful for the change that had taken place in his dear son, who was now roaming around with a brilliant sort of headgear and black *achkan*[1] looking very smart like a local feudal. He said: 'I'll now be able to put him up for an interview for the army.' Barrie said: 'I'm afraid not, because he's changed so much, he'd probably get court-martialled.' And that was the change in my life.

Unlike the traditional Indian centres of religious learning, the British Indian schools brought children of different castes and religious communities together in the same classrooms and dormitories, taught them a common language and, in some cases, gave them their first taste of European racial arrogance. Despite the entry of growing numbers of Indians, these schools continued to be dominated by teachers and pupils from the 'Anglo-Indian' community, people of mixed race who nevertheless regarded themselves as white. Their own racial ambivalence often

[1] A long, knee-length formal coat.

made them more British than the British, and more prejudiced against Indians. Renuka Ray, who started her schooling in England, felt the contrast when she returned to Calcutta to become one of the few Indian girls at its leading convent school.

About 1911 or 1912 we were in England for a couple of years. I was about seven or eight years old, and we went to the Kensington High School in London. It was a very happy two years. The children were all very nice, and in those days we never knew that there was such a thing as colour prejudice. Later, when I came back to India, my father was posted in a district where there was no high school for girls, and I was put as a boarder at Loretto House in Calcutta. It was then that I first began to realise what is known as colour discrimination. Those were the years when the First World War was on, and English people who normally sent their children abroad were sending them to Loretto House. And there were the 'Anglo-Indians' who were also included among them. I myself and one or two other Indian girls were discriminated against by them, though not by the nuns who were mostly Irish and behaved very nicely with us. My grandfather, who was then Chief Inspector of Schools, was a very fair-skinned Indian, and he came to the school. Before he went away, I and my cousin were sent for to speak to him. Afterwards, the girls said: 'Why were you sent for?' I said: 'He is my grandfather.' 'He can't be!' said they, 'because, after all, he's an Englishman!' We laughed at them, but one could see the colour prejudice.

Many Indians swallowed their racial pride and accepted second-class treatment as the price of becoming 'Brown Englishmen'. But there were others in whom the awareness of discrimination produced rebellious reactions and a determination to excel. Aruna Asaf Ali, a future nationalist leader, recalls her first clash with British authority as a schoolgirl in the 1920s.

When I went to All Saints College in Naini Tal, it began with a little struggle. I was by then about fourteen, and I'd just decided to do away with frocks and get into saris. I went marching up and told the Principal: 'I've just given up frocks. At this age Indian parents don't like their children to wear frocks. Up to eleven or twelve it's all right.' At first, she said: 'No, we can't waive the rule.' I went back, and I grumbled, and I wrote to her again, and ultimately she agreed. I thought it was a great personal victory, I didn't understand the politics of it then, but here it was, my first confrontation with a British lady. Then other Indian girls also gradually switched over to saris.

The feeling that we were a less cultured people was driven into us by the 'Anglo-Indian' girls, that they belonged to a civilised country whereas we were barbarians. That was the atmosphere. We were children; we liked each other; we became friends; but on and off it would just pop up. For instance, there was a limerick. It started with, 'The poor benighted Hindu ... this is all he can do'. That upset me completely when I read it, and I felt very ashamed. I didn't know what to do or say about it. I wasn't grown up enough politically. I swallowed it, but it rankled in my mind. And that gave us a complex: let's teach them that we are not inferior.

Those were times when our parents were very keen that we go to good schools, that we must know good English, correct English, correct accent. It mustn't be the Indian accent, the Babu[1] English. That thing was driven into us – you must talk correct King's English. Our curriculum, right from the Bible down to history, was patterned on the British system. I particularly fell in love with English literature. I remember one of my teachers said: 'You're good at English, you've got a good ear. You must choose English teaching as your career. You must go to Oxford and take a degree there.' So that feeling, that I could go to Oxford, seemed to me the pinnacle of ambition, and I lived with that thought for a long time. But we didn't belong to a very affluent family, so there was no question of affording it.

Looking back today at their Anglo-Indian education, many western-ised Indians admit to a sense of loss about the extent to which they were cut off from their own cultural roots. 'We were really turned into the children of colonialism,' says Romesh Thapar. 'We had skills. I don't deny all the skills I developed with a man like Barrie. . . . But it deprived me of my contact with my own cultural past, which I have had to pick up largely through English. If I had had a basic Sanskrit education and followed that up with a much greater stress on the mother-tongue, was able to read literature in the mother-tongue, I think I would be very much better equipped to understand my country.' Khushwant Singh, another prominent English-language journalist, also complains: 'The emphasis on English did cut me off from Punjabi and Urdu, which were my languages, and I had to relearn them, almost, after I returned from England.'

Western-educated Indians like Tagore may have led the rediscovery and revival of Indian cultural traditions; but they had to swim against the prevailing tide to do so. Rukmini Devi Arundale, an Indian woman who married an Englishman, presided for half a century over the revival of South Indian dance and music at the Kalakshetra arts academy in Madras. Shortly before her death in the spring of 1986, she was still bitter about the negative effects of Anglo-Indian education and culture.

There were many enlightened Englishmen from very cultured families, very artistic in their own way. My husband was a musician and a composer, too, and his family were painters. But they were not aware of Indian art. . . . When I was in school, there was a very good teacher of Indian music. There was also a very good Western

---

1 Derogatory term for Indian clerks.

musician. The western music was compulsory for all of us; the Indian music was not compulsory. So all the students learnt the Western music, and they didn't learn the Indian. I was one of the few that did. . . . And I remember it because I come from a musical family and felt very much this lack of attention.

English-medium convent schools were the main stepping-stone to the universities at which Indians studied the new professional and commercial disciplines that the Raj introduced. The three great universities of British India – Bombay, Madras and Calcutta – were established in 1857, on the eve of traditional India's final and unsuccessful revolt against British rule. With their neo-Gothic spires and stained-glass windows, they made a brave attempt to conjure up the ethos of distant Oxford and Cambridge. Professor G. C. Bannerji, a former principal of Bombay's Elphinstone College, recalls his own student days at the Deccan College in Poona.

The Deccan College had very much the same physical features as an Oxford College. For instance, there was a college building, there were hostels, and some of the rooms in the college building were given to hostel students. I lived in one of them for a short period. There were young Englishmen who came out from England who took classes; and they sometimes took individual students as they did in Oxford. And one of them wrote home: 'I've finished my teaching, so I'll go down to the river and meet another fellow whom I'll teach how to row.'

Another Englishman whom I remember very well was a man called Wodehouse, a brother of P. G. Wodehouse. Sometimes he used to ask us: 'Have you seen my brother's latest rubbish?' He was a very fine scholar, who won the Newdigate Prize for the best poem of the year, and he was an original thinker. . . . We were walking through the library once when we came to the Elizabethan dramatists. He looked at them and said: 'These you take your hat off to, but you don't really read them.'

Professor K. Swaminathan recalls similar attempts to emulate British academic life at Madras University.

When I joined the Presidency College, Madras, in 1912, most of the professors were Englishmen or Scotsmen; there was only one Indian professor. We didn't see much difference between the English professors and their Indian assistants. They were all friendly and took as much interest in us as our own uncles. . . . Racial difference and so on might be there in the political or commercial sphere; but in education most Englishmen who came out as teachers, whether in missionary or government colleges, were quite friendly. I remember a man called Douglas, whose brother was in the ICS and was murdered in Calcutta. When I went to condole with him, he said: 'It's a bad system. He was a good man, but he paid the price for being in a bad system.' Such was his generosity and broadmindedness. He was a wonderful man. And there were many such people.

The standards they tried to maintain were those of Oxford and Cambridge; and they did, I think manage to maintain those standards. . . . We tried to follow the same syllabuses, the same courses of study, and prescribed the same textbooks. For example, as a student I studied Gothic, Old English, Middle English and so on.

In such surroundings, with British mentors who were often remarkably enlightened, young Indians discovered an England that was a world apart from the bureaucracy of Anglo-India – the England of Shakespeare and Wordsworth. As the poet Harindranath Chattopadhyaya reminds us, it was possible to reject the Empire while embracing its language and literature.

I didn't choose English; English chose me. I took to English as a duck takes to water. When I was a very young boy, my father insisted that I should learn English side by side with Urdu. And the English language has flowed through me, and I seem to be acquainted with the nuances of the words. . . . When I was hardly eleven, I used to read Shakespeare aloud, although I couldn't understand the words. I certainly knew that I was climbing a mountain, and it was wonderful doing it. . . . I loved Milton, although I couldn't understand him either. . . . Shelley has meant a lot to me. In fact, I sometimes feel that I could write a book on Shelley, such a book that very few could write, because I know Shelley, every word of what he's written, the colouring. I feel one with him.

In the colonial context, Shakespeare and Shelley did not become an escape from political reality, and the British Indian universities could not long remain mere academic ivory towers. The more avidly Indian students consumed British and European literature and political classics, the more warmly they accepted Western notions of political freedom and national self-determination, the more difficult it became to justify the despotism of the Raj as a system so alien to Britain's own liberal traditions. The oldest and most venerable educational establishments of the Raj were also among the first to become the cradles of India's new nationalism. And the Indians who quoted Shakespeare most enthusiastically were often the first to raise the banner of revolt against British rule.

88

CRADLES OF NATIONALISM

The relations between those of us who were politically activist and the British professors were particularly warm; because it seemed to us that they rather liked us for being as cheeky as we were and not being very docile.

M. R. Masani *(former nationalist politician)*

In 1911 British India had 186 colleges of higher education attended by just over 36,000 students. By 1939, the number of colleges had doubled, while the number of Indians in higher education had leapt up fourfold to 145,000. It was not accidental that this rapid expansion of college education coincided with the rise of an increasingly militant and broad-based nationalist movement. Large numbers of students, drawn together by collegiate life and exposed to the most advanced political ideas, were the natural power-base of a movement led predominantly by urban, middle-class politicians.

By the 1920s it was clear that the very education with which the Raj had hoped to train loyal Indian subordinates had turned against it in the demand for self-government. This development was not altogether unexpected. It had been anticipated in the fierce debate between the protagonists and opponents of Western education during the first half of the nineteenth century; and Britain's more enlightened colonial educationists had always welcomed the prospect of Indians some day graduating through British education to democratic self-government. What they had not anticipated was that the pace and manner of India's political graduation might be beyond British control.

British Indian universities, of course, did not set out to encourage political activity. Most colleges were owned by government and staffed, in the early years, by teachers who were either apolitical or proud of their imperial mission. The academic syllabus, with its old-fashioned emulation of British models, certainly did not emphasise India's national heritage. The stress was on European literature and history; and India's own past was studied largely in terms of the achievements of successive British governor-generals. And yet political awareness could not be confined within the limits of British Indian textbooks, especially as the teaching profession was itself being Indianised with the entry of growing numbers of fresh graduates, most of whom were at least sympathetic to the nationalist cause.

Miss Shiva Dua, the retired principal of a Delhi women's college, was one of the new generation of Indian teachers who grew up amid the nationalist fervour of the 1920s and '30s. She remembers how, as a young history lecturer in the early 1940s, she agonised over whether to compromise her nationalist principles and take a job with a government college. Her experience had been coloured by the protest resignation of one of her own teachers, the daughter of a prominent nationalist leader.

> When I was a student in the first year, Mrs Sarojini Naidu's daughter, Leelamani Naidu, was a lecturer in the college, and she taught us philosophy. During one of the lectures, Miss Naidu opened the door and found the Principal standing there. She banged the door against the Principal and came and thumped the table and said: 'If this lady thinks that I am preaching sedition and she's trying to eavesdrop, she's mistaken. If she thinks that, because I'm the daughter of my mother, I'm preaching sedition, she's wrong. But children, don't be surprised if you don't find me here after the summer vacation. If I can't have freedom of conscience in teaching, I shall not serve the government.' So she went. That incident had an impression on me, and I felt that if philosophy can't be taught, then history is really going to be interfered with. So I decided never to go to a government college to teach, and taught in private institutions without any remuneration.

After a spell of voluntary work, Miss Dua decided that she could be more useful to the cause of nationalist education inside the official system. She found a job at the same college in Lahore where she had been a student and opted to lecture in British and European history, which she thought would involve less compromises than the teaching of Indian history. She soon discovered that even a colonial curriculum could be turned to nationalist ends.

> Talking to the students about Magna Carta – 1215 – I tried to draw a pen-picture for them of how, at Runnymede, the people sat and forced King John to sign the Magna Carta. I said: 'If a king, your own king, can be made to do this, what can be done for an alien government? If John had not been their own king, I don't know what else they would have done.' Then, similarly, I used the [British] Civil War and said: 'Look, Charles had to pay with his head, and if he were a foreigner I don't know what else he might have had to do.' And American history also – the question of how the colonies broke away, the No-Tax campaign that they raised and the Declaration of Freedom. . . . English literature also; Shakespeare belonging to the Elizabethan age, and how much of his literature stresses patriotism.

Alongside the history of European revolutions, Indian students were also imbibing the more homespun teachings of Mahatma Gandhi. By relating Western-style nationalism to the traditional symbols of rural India, Gandhi offered westernised Indian youth the opportunity to overcome their sense of cultural alienation and strike new roots that were specifically Indian. His call for non-cooperation with the Raj included a boycott of government schools and colleges. In the course of his civil disobedience campaigns in the 1920s and '30s, thousands of Indian students stayed away from classes, enrolled as Congress volunteers and courted arrest in nationalist demonstrations. The *Swadeshi* campaign, an almost religious crusade against British goods, was particularly successful in capturing the imagination of Indian youth. Shiva Dua describes the spirit of romantic sacrifice that it aroused in her and many others of her generation.

My eldest sister was in the movement itself, and she wore nothing but *khadi*.[1] Since I was being brought up by her, having lost my mother at the age of three, I was under her influence, and she gave me only *khadi* to wear. When I went to school. I found everybody else wearing very fine foreign clothes, but it didn't affect me at all. I felt proud that I was the only child in a whole college of 600 children who was wearing *khadi*, and I felt I was something very different from the others. . . . In 1930, Mahatma Gandhi gave his call that foreign clothes should be burnt. The students' union in Lahore decided to go and collect foreign clothes from the city and have a bonfire. And they passed our house with the slogans 'Boycott foreign clothes', 'Burn foreign clothes'. There was hardly anything foreign in our house; but Mother's belongings were still there, and one sari had come to me as my share of Mother's belongings. I wore it a couple of times with a kind of mental conflict going on over whether it should be worn or not. There were pulls in two different directions, but I had kept it very sentimentally, keeping it preserved. When the call came, and the crowd was just below our house, and the neighbours were throwing them things, immediately I decided that Mother was Mother, but the Mother Country was higher than Mother, and the sari must go, and I gave it.

Bonfires of foreign clothes were only a symbolic beginning; but they were a form of direct action which appealed particularly to Indian women. The cause of female emancipation had already reached the stage when it was becoming common for middle-class families to send their daughters to school and college. Gandhi carried the process further by singling out women as the ideal passive resisters, better equipped than men to practise his particular brand of non-violent protest. Women students responded in growing numbers to his call, followed by even larger numbers of illiterate, rural women. But whether you were man, woman or child, Gandhian non-violence included a readiness to face and overcome police violence, as Usha Mehta, then a young schoolgirl, recalls.

I remember the year 1928, when the Simon Commission was touring the country in connection with constitutional reforms. All the parties were in favour of boycotting the Commission, and the slogan that was very much in the air was 'Simon, Go Back!' We

[1] Hand-spun and hand-woven cloth, the wearing of which became mandatory for all Congress members.

children also felt attracted to the movement, and we formed the *Vanar Sena* or Monkey Army. This was the volunteer corps in which mostly boys were involved. We girls felt that we must have an identity of our own, so we formed a separate Cat Army or *Manjar Sena*. We used to take out processions and shout slogans like 'Vande Mataram' ['I bow to thee, my motherland'], 'Inqilab Zindabad' ['Long live the revolution'], 'Up, up the national flag, Down, down the Union Jack'.

One day I remember we were marching with the [Congress] tricolour in our hands. From the opposite direction, came the police with their *lathis*,[1] and we became victims of a *lathi*-charge. One volunteer fell down unconscious, and the flag also fell from her hands. We felt very unhappy, because we had not been able to keep the honour of the flag. So we asked our elders to show us a way out. When they could not do anything, we said: 'Please do what we want you to do.' We made them open the *khadi* shops in the middle of the night and take out *khadi* cloth in the three colours of the flag: white, red and green. Overnight all the volunteers of the Cat Army sat down on the streets and stitched uniforms in the three colours of the flag. The next morning we took out a procession, and all of us were dressed in white *chunnis* [headscarves], red petticoats and green blouses. We had no flag in our hands, but we were throwing a challenge to the police and telling them that today, if you have the courage, you see how you can bring down our flag. Because we had become live flags, and unless the police shot us it would not have been possible for them to dishonour the flag.

For most young Indians, a less dramatic but more direct encounter with British authority took the form of challenging the discipline imposed by British principals. Shiva Dua can look back on a series of such undergraduate battles, which began with a decision by herself and other students to mourn the execution of the revolutionary leader, Bhagat Singh, in March 1931.

That was a time when the whole country was simmering with anger and agitation. All we could do was to let the Principal know that we too suffered the same kind of agony that the nation had been made to suffer. We decided to put on black clothes on the day after the execution, and we asked the washermen who lived on the premises to dye black veils for us. The Principal came to know; and she went and threatened the washermen with being thrown out and removed the entire 80 veils that were to be dyed black. So I went and collected a bale of about 100 veils, sent them to an outside dyer, and in the morning I took them to college. The entire hall was dressed in black, some in black saris and blouses, others in black veils. . . . It was a surprise for the Principal to find

---

1 Long, wooden staves, tipped with metal.

the entire hall absolutely black, but she never uttered a word. We wore that black for thirteen days,[1] most of us.

A year later Miss Dua found herself at the centre of another confrontation with the Principal, this time over the singing of the nationalist anthem, '*Vande Mataram*', at the annual college prize-distribution.

It occurred to some of us that we should ask the Principal to allow us to sing '*Vande Mataram*' along with 'God Save the King'. She was absolutely adamant, and she refused. We felt very hurt, and we tried to explain to her that there was nothing seditious about singing '*Vande Mataram*'. But she said: 'No, that's politics.' So we kept quiet and decided not to participate in the singing of 'God Save the King'. A few prize-winners – I was one of them – were sitting on the front benches. We decided that when they stand up for 'God Save the King', we'll just keep sitting; and we just kept sitting. The Principal was so furious, she turned red; and we just refused to look at her. I don't know why she had the feeling that I was at the bottom of it. But at the end of the ceremony, she called me to her office and said: 'Shiva, I didn't expect this from you.' I said: 'Have I done anything wrong by expressing a love for my mother-country?' She said nothing and just kept quiet. Thereafter, I had a feeling that my career would be affected, that she would never allow me to come back to the college in the third year. But I confess with great pride and admiration for the Principal that, not only did she accept me, but when she found that I had come out from the examination with very good results and that I had won a merit scholarship, she wrote a letter of congratulations and said: 'I hope you are coming back to your college.' And I went back to my college very happily.

When Shiva Dua went on to take her MA at the Government College, Lahore, she was equally defiant of attempts by the Principal there to curb her political activities.

The Principal was a retired army man who had taken part in the First World War. He was also head of the History Department and taught us British constitutional history. In 1935, the All India Students' Conference was going to take place in Lahore, and also a poetic symposium, to which Mrs Sarojini Naidu was coming. We students of the university were organising the reception committee and selling tickets for it. I was one of the active workers, and the Principal sent for me. I knew why he was sending for me, but I didn't realise he would be so angry just because I was enrolling members for the reception committee of the Students' Conference. He took out a document which I had signed and which every student was made to sign while being admitted to the Government College. It said: 'I solemnly declare that I shall not take part in

1 The traditional Hindu period of mourning.

politics while I am a student here.' He showed it to me and said: 'Is that your signature?' I said: 'Yes, sir.' 'Will you read out the declaration?' he said. So I read it out. He said: 'Now, you are going back on what you have said.' I said: 'No, sir.' 'You are working for the Students' Conference?' he asked. I said: 'Yes, but that's not politics. It's part of our student activities.' He said: 'You know the consequences. It can mean rustication. Are you prepared for it?' 'Yes, sir, I am,' I said, 'if you are prepared to face the hornet's nest that you would raise by rusticating me or anybody else.' 'What would your people feel?' he asked. 'My people will be very happy', I replied, 'because they didn't want me to go for the Master's. I had to fight a battle with them to come and do my Master's. So if you throw me out, they won't mind. But the trouble will be for you.' After that, he just said: 'You can go,' and I went out. We all decided outside that, while previously we had decided to enrol ten members each, we'd now have to have fifteen members each. We all threw ourselves, heart and soul, into this; and the Principal never said anything to us.

British tolerance of Indian student politics varied considerably between different colleges and universities. In general, university authorities were less sympathetic to Indian nationalism than they might have been, because they disliked the religiosity and apparent obscurantism of Gandhian politics. But while few British academics encouraged student activism, many were fierce in their defence of academic freedom from government interference. Professor G. C. Bannerji remembers as a student being impressed with the way the British principal of the Deccan College in Poona dealt with police officers who wanted to search the campus for alleged terrorists.

F. T. Bain became principal of the college at a time when, politically, there was a lot of planned violence. One of the district collectors was shot at, and they came to search the Deccan College, because they believed that the man who had been planning it was staying in the hostel. The news reached Bain. He came down, met the police officer and said: 'Please get out immediately. This is my territory. You give me a complaint. I will take down a reply from the student if he is here, and then I will recommend the necessary disciplinary measures to the appropriate authorities.' They respected his point of view, and they withdrew.

At an institution like Bombay's Elphinstone College, with its long tradition of political liberalism, relations between nationalist students and their British teachers could be even warmer. Professor Bannerji, himself a former principal of the college, describes how his distinguished British predecessor, Principal Hamill, handled youthful unrest.

He was a very vivid personality, one of those men who are interested in students as human beings. He made friends with a large number of students, to the extent of knowing what their individual problems were. He was there for a short time when the Quit India movement[1] was on and, as was perhaps to be expected, the movement was at its most intense in Elphinstone College. We as staff were in a very ambiguous position. I used to meet Hamill sometimes, and he'd say: 'Yes, this chap, he's had a bad love affair, and he thinks that he must pour out his soul in the Quit India movement. They all come to me.'

According to Bannerji, this human approach meant that, even when student protest took violent forms, the college authorities would not have dreamt of handing over offenders to the police.

One day, under the lecturer's platform in a science lecture-hall, we found a bomb. We informed the police; they came, handled it very gingerly, put it into a bucket of water and then opened it up. The water began bubbling, so there must have been some very potent stuff inside it. We knew, or had a strong suspicion, who had done it; but they didn't ask us to name the person, and we didn't. In fact, it was an embarrassing situation for all of us — teachers, students and also the police.

Principal Hamill presided over the most formative years of several generations of Elphinstonians, many of whom went on to prominent roles in public life. One of the college's oldest surviving alumni, M. R. Masani, an undergraduate of the 1920s, confirms that the relationship that he and other student radicals had with their British lecturers was one of mutual respect.

We stood up to them and refused to allow them to bully us or shout us down; and soon they appreciated this and became friends with us. . . . Professor Hamill actually picked out one or two of us who were outspoken nationalists and seemed to enjoy talking to us. I remember he took us out in a sailing-boat more than once, so that we could be out in the open and chat freely with him, without any of the inhibitions which would have been there in his office in college. He seemed to rather enjoy talking to the young rebels.

There were some British lecturers who went beyond mere friendliness, like Christopher Ackroyd of St Paul's College in Calcutta. He was an ordained clergyman who nevertheless wore *khaddar*[2] and seemed more interested in winning converts to Marxism than to Christianity. C. Sehanabish, a veteran member of the Communist Party of India, remembers falling under his spell as a student in 1934.

He was a very strange Englishman, in the sense that he used to put on a *khaddar pajama*[3] and *khaddar punjabi*[4] and go about

1 The final and most violent confrontation between Congress and the Raj, launched in August 1942.
2 Another word for *khadi*, the hand-spun and hand-woven cloth worn by Congress members.
3 Loose, Indian-style trousers.
4 A knee-length shirt.

barefoot on the Calcutta streets and only had a *khaddar chadar*[1]
over his body during the winter. He used to lie on a bench which
was much too short for him – he was six foot two inches tall – and
his legs used to protrude out of it. I took with him a class on *Wage-
Labour and Capital*, Marx's book. Till that time, I had never found a
library so well equipped with Marxist and progressive literature. His
other hobby was a very beautiful collection of Western music and
records. He influenced me greatly. He asked me: 'Why are you
reading Marxism? Do you want to become a political worker, or is
this just to add to your knowledge?' I said that I certainly wanted to
do something. Then he said: 'If you want to do something, I think
you should be with the mainstream of the Communist movement.'

Ackroyd himself fell foul of the British authorities when he decided to
investigate the shooting of two political prisoners in a police detention
camp. In an attempt to break what he thought was a conspiracy of silence,
he sent his findings to the London *Times*, which published them in an
article. Although the authorities retaliated by getting him transferred to
Kanpur in the United Provinces, that did not prevent him from throwing
himself into trade union activities there.

The British Left had an even greater influence on Indians who went to
university in England. The London School of Economics, in particular, did
more than any Indian college to radicalise a whole generation of nationalist leaders. Renuka Ray, a minister in post-independence Congress
governments, is proud of her political apprenticeship at the LSE in the
1920s.

When I was told by my father that I was to go abroad for my studies, I
was very resentful at first. I was then with Gandhiji at his *ashram* at
Sabarmati; and Gandhiji told me: 'You must go, because in England
it will be different. I have been educated there myself, and it's a free
atmosphere, and you must take advantage of it.'

I'm grateful that he and my father insisted on my going to the LSE.
Some of the people who were notable in British politics later were
our lecturers. It was 1923 or so, and there was a general election, and
some of our lecturers were actually standing for election. It was my
first experience of electioneering, and I was rather surprised because
the women, particularly in London, were not interested in voting. It
was only by persuading them and doing a bit of baby-sitting for them
that some of them came out. And this in a country where women –
the Pankhursts in particular – had done so much.

I was socialist-inclined before I went to the LSE; but certainly
Harold Laski, in particular, had a great deal to do with my becoming
knowledgeable about things which I used to speak about but actually
knew little about before that. . . . It was a stimulating atmosphere.
The LSE was like a miniature UN, and the exchange of ideas with
some of the most brilliant minds did help us a great deal.

1 A sheet or shawl.

Major Attlee[1] was my adviser for studies, because I was doing Public Administration and he was a lecturer in that subject. Very much later, when he came to India, I was a minister in the West Bengal Cabinet. We were together at a banquet at Government House, and afterwards he sat next to me and said: 'I used to know a Miss Mukherji who was a student of mine. Do you know how I can get in touch with her?' I said: 'If you will make a discount for the years that have gone by and for the weight that I have put on, you might recognise Miss Mukherji.' He was thrilled to hear that his pupil had become a minister, and after that he mentioned it at many of his meetings.

By the 1930s, British Communists had replaced Labour politicians as the ideological mentors of Indian students abroad. They were the channel of communication between left-wing groups in India and the Communist International in Moscow; and it was a time when many Indians saw Stalin's Russia as the only international challenge to the British empire, on the one hand, and the new, fascist Axis, on the other. Some prominent leaders of the British Communist Party had special links with India – Ben Bradley, who had suffered imprisonment in India for helping to set up Communist trade unions; R. Palme Dutt, who was half-Indian by birth; and Shapurji Saklatvala or 'Comrade Sak', an Indian who was elected MP for Battersea North in the 1920s. They were active in setting up Marxist study-circles and activist 'cells' among the Indian student community, with the aim of recruiting and training a nucleus of brilliant, young Communists who would return to lead the Indian revolution. Several of India's most prominent Communist politicians won their political spurs in London, in the student campaigns of the 1930s. They include the present Marxist Chief Minister of West Bengal, Jyoti Basu, who was in London from 1935 to 1939 studying Law at the Middle Temple.

When I first went there, I was not in politics at all in India, either in the student movement or anywhere else. My family was not a political family. But there, within one year, I came in touch with Marxist literature and also with some leaders of the Communist Party of Great Britain. I was particularly attracted to the Communist Party, because that was the one party which was talking about Indian freedom. They were trying to form groups of Indians in Cambridge, Oxford, London and some other cities to give Communist ideas to students.

Those were very stirring years, with the Japanese invasion of China, then Abyssinia being invaded by Mussolini. The rise of Hitler had already taken place, and he was on the warpath. And then the Spanish Civil War. . . . I remember that at that time there was the rise of a fascist party in Great Britain also. We often used to hear them at street-corner meetings and try and ask them all sorts of inconvenient questions.

1 Clement Attlee, the future Labour Prime Minister.

For some Indians, student life in London also brought a shared experience of racial prejudice. 'There was colour prejudice, but not very openly,' says Jyoti Basu. 'We could find it when we went to hunt for digs. They didn't insult us, but we knew that it was because of colour that we couldn't rent the place.' Another left-wing law student, S. K. Acharyya, who later served Mr Basu's government as its Advocate-General,[1] remembered acquiring a sense of racial solidarity with other Third World peoples during his student years in London. 'Just before I went to England,' he recalled, 'the Abyssinian War had ended. We felt terribly shocked at the way the Italians bombed the whole of Abyssinia. And being also black, naturally that influenced us a lot.'

When young radicals like Basu and Acharyya returned from England to the political fray in India, they flocked to the banner of a growing left-wing revolt against Mahatma Gandhi's leadership of Congress. The Communist Party of India, founded in the 1920s, and the Congress Socialist Party, founded in 1934, were launched and led by British-educated Fabian and Marxist intellectuals, who retained strong links with their ideological mentors in the British Labour and Communist movements. And although they rejected Gandhi's non-violence and demanded a class war against imperialism and its Indian collaborators, one thing which many left-wing leaders shared with the Mahatma was an education which had left them too British to ever really hate the British.

1 The Indian equivalent of the British Attorney-General.

Top: *An Indian Ascot –
upper-class Indians mingling
with British spectators at the
main annual racing event in
Karachi, 1937.*

Above: *British and Indian
guests at a princely banquet.*

Right: *A south Indian Christian family. Early missionaries urged their converts to give up Indian habits and culture.*
Below: *Indian teachers and 'Bible-women' trained by a Christian mission.*
Far right: *Sir Rabindranath Tagore (1861–1941) led a cultural renaissance which tried to combine Eastern and Western learning.*
Below right: *Theosophist leader, Dr Annie Besant, with Indian nationalists in Bombay, 1923. She brought her experience of the Irish Home Rule movement to the Indian National Congress, over which she presided.*

Top: *Cricket at the Lawrence School in the Punjab Hills. Founded in the nineteenth century for the children of British and 'Anglo-Indian' soldiers, it remains one of India's leading boarding schools.*

Above: *The hockey team at Aitchison College, Lahore, a centre of Western education for the feudal nobility of Punjab. Known as 'India's Eton', it was famous for its sporting achievements.*

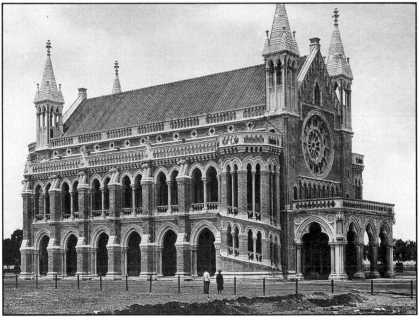

Top: *Elphinstone College,
Bombay, one of the earliest
institutions of Western higher
education, was founded by
Indians in 1827 and named
after an enlightened British
governor.*

Above: *The convocation hall of
Bombay University, founded in
1857, was famous for its
stained glass rose-window.
British Indian universities
tried hard to emulate the
architecture and academic
standards of Oxbridge.*

Left: *Mahatma Gandhi as a young, British-trained barrister in a pork-pie hat and Edwardian suit, c. 1903.*
Below far left: *Aruna Asaf Ali, romantic heroine of the Quit India underground movement, with her husband, a prominent Congress Muslim, 1947.*
Below left: *Jawaharlal Nehru (centre) and Subhas Bose (right) were both Cambridge-educated nationalists, but held very different views on how to fight the British.*
Right: *Kamladevi Chattopadhyaya, wife of the poet Harindranath, leading a women's demonstration against the Raj. Gandhi's campaigns drew thousands of Indian women out of their traditional seclusion.*
Below right: *Police with* lathis *confronting nationalist demonstrators in 1932. Gandhian non-violence required a willingness to suffer* lathi-*blows without retaliation.*

Top: *The building designed by Sir Edwin Lutyens for the élite Legislative Assembly of the Raj now houses independent India's Parliament in New Delhi.*

Above: *Beating Retreat (New Delhi, January 1986), performed amid the splendour of Lutyens's viceregal capital, is still an annual reminder of India's surprisingly fond farewell to empire.*

ANGER WITHOUT HATRED

That was Gandhiji's greatness – that he realised that the British were Christian gentlemen trying to play cricket. And Gandhiji played the game according to their own rules. Of course, if the Soviets or the Nazis had been there, they would have executed Gandhiji long before he came effective; but the British played ball with him. Gandhiji was shrewd enough to utilise the nature of British rule in India to extort independence without very much bloodshed.

M. R. Masani *(General Secretary of the Congress Socialist Party, 1934–39)*

Compared with most other independence struggles, India's was remarkably free of violence or rancour. While the credit goes largely to Gandhi's non-violence, the Mahatma himself was no historical accident. He was a London-trained barrister, schooled in British legal and constitutional theory; and his creed of *Satyagraha*, or the Path of Truth, owed at least as much to the Christian pacifism of his missionary and Quaker friends as to the ancient Hindu concept of *Ahimsa* (non-violence). Shorn of its religious trappings, Gandhian non-violence was also a pragmatic political tactic which recognised British military superiority in India and the futility of another armed revolt like that of 1857.

Gandhi's metamorphosis from a young Victorian lawyer, who danced, drank and wore three-piece suits, into the familiar, half-naked ascetic of popular legend was as much a political as a spiritual homecoming. While his saintly aura enabled him to tap the strong Hindu revivalism of his time, his secular background and education made him an acceptable father-figure to many of the younger and more radical generation of nationalists. One of them, Aruna Asaf Ali, was a westernised Hindu woman who married a leading Congress Muslim and eventually became a prominent left-wing politician in her own right. She describes how she and other young socialists accepted Gandhi as their political leader, while taking his spiritual fads with a pinch of salt.

To follow Gandhi's insistence on no smoking, no drinking, the vow of celibacy, abstinence and the simple life – by and large, I don't think our types, the westernised Congressmen, ever took to it. . . . Gandhiji was a very peculiar fascination for us. We could not accept all that he wanted us to do; it seemed very hard; but what we could do, we did. For instance, giving up foreign cloth: it was a bit of a struggle to do it, but we gave it up. Giving up jewellery; anyway, jewellery had never fascinated me for long. Being prepared for any sacrifice – non-violent struggle means no retaliation, and you must be prepared for all the hardship this resistance might cause – that was the basic political education for me.

Even the ascetic rigours of Gandhian *ashram* life had their charm for those more accustomed to Western comforts, as Renuka Ray, a London-educated nationalist, confesses.

Everybody told me: 'You'll find it terrible, and the food is awful.' But I was young, and I enjoyed it. We used to get up early in the morning at 5.30 and bathe in the river. Everybody had to be on time; but some of us used to try and be truants. . . . When you are young, something novel can be exciting. It was quite a thrill to me at that time.

For Indians in search of cultural roots, Gandhi, like his artistic contemporary, Tagore, seemed to offer an authentic synthesis of East and West. According to Usha Mehta, now Director of the Gandhi Museum in Bombay, the Mahatma may have rejected superficial European fashions of dress and social etiquette, but he revered the more fundamental Western values of self-reliance and political freedom.

I first went to Gandhiji's *ashram* with my parents when I was hardly six or seven. Gandhiji was going for prayers, so we also had to attend the prayers; and it was only after the prayers were over that he met us. Prayers were regularly held every day in the morning and evening, and this had its own effect on us. The simplicity of the community life that all the ashramites were leading impressed me very deeply. Everyone there had to look after his own work, clean his own utensils, wash his own clothes; and so all those who stayed in the *ashram* were made to learn self-dependence. This attracted me very much. . . . It was in keeping with our ancient Indian traditions.

For Aruna Asaf Ali, Gandhi's religiosity evoked, not so much ancient Hinduism, but the Christian imagery she had imbibed at her convent school.

He was the magnetic type; he just drew us, and he talked to us in a quiet, gentle manner. The atmosphere was very simple, very rustic, and it seemed to me like an Indian monastery. I'd read a lot about the monastic orders and how austere they were, the nuns and fathers, in the Roman Catholic church; and Gandhi had that kind of religiousness. When he used to hold his prayer-meetings, what helped me to understand him instantly was his insistence on singing hymns from all the religions – from the Hindu scriptures, the Koran and Christianity. 'Lead Kindly Light' was his favourite hymn. . . . He had all the attributes which Christ was supposed to have, particularly the quiet way in which he spoke about the poor. . . . There were many things that we had read and heard about Christ that fitted in with Gandhiji's own teachings – the way he spoke, his sorrow, and sometimes his anger-filled voice.

Gandhi's saintly charisma had a particular appeal for Indian women, and not only for educated, middle-class women, as Aruna Asaf Ali reminds us.

Gandhiji's appeal was something elemental. At last, a woman was made to feel the equal of man; that feeling dominated us all, educated and non-educated. The majority of women who came into the struggle were not educated or westernised.... The real liberation or emancipation of Indian women can be traced to this period, the 1930s. Earlier, there had been many influences at work, many social reformers had gone ahead, it was all in the air. But no one single act could have done what Gandhiji did when he first called upon women to join and said: 'They are the better symbols of mankind. They have all the virtues of a *satyagrahi*.'[1] All that puffed us up enormously and gave us a great deal of self-confidence.

Another female activist, Usha Mehta, remembers the impact on even the older women of her family when Gandhi launched his civil disobedience campaign in 1930 with a symbolic protest against the government monopoly of salt.

Gandhiji was a great emancipator.... I remember, during the Salt *Satyagraha*, many women of all ages came out to join the movement. Even our old aunts and great-aunts and grandmothers used to bring pitchers of salt water to their houses and manufacture illegal salt. And then they would shout at the top of their voices: 'We have broken the Salt Law!'

For many young women like herself, says Miss Mehta, Gandhian civil disobedience also provided an alternative to conventional marriage and domesticity.

My father was progressive, and I would have gone to college and pursued a university education in any case. But our family being traditional, perhaps I would have been compelled to get married and lead a settled life. Because of my involvement with the struggle, I not only went to jail in 1942, but also pursued a career of my own. This is how Gandhiji led women to assert their rights.

The left wing of Congress never fully accepted Gandhi's creed of non-violence. But many of those who argued that revolutionary violence was necessary to counter the violence of the state joined the Mahatma in disowning any racial hatred of the British. For instance, Aruna Asaf Ali, who led violent underground resistance to the British in the 1940s, admits that people like herself were so steeped in British ways that even their favourite bedtime reading was Agatha Christie.

We were angered; something angered us, and that was the sense of humiliation. But there was never any hatred, because one was so attuned to the British culture by our education. All the leadership,

1 A follower of *Satyagraha*, Gandhi's non violent creed.

including Gandhiji and Nehru, had spent their early years in England. They were all influenced by British thought, British revolutionary ideas, and therefore European also. I read a great deal of all those exciting books about the French Revolution. The French Revolution and the British struggle – during Cromwell's period and subsequently – made us feel that they in their country have fought tyranny in their own way, so we will do the same. That is why our leaders were always telling the British: 'How can you do these things? They're against your own basic values.' We had no hatred. In fact, it was the other way round – it was their values which made us revolt.

With leadership of this kind, nationalist campaigns could be a chivalrous and even amicable contest with the authorities, as M. R. Masani recalls.

I cannot complain of any personal unpleasantness or bad behaviour. When I courted arrest in January 1933, by presiding over an illegal meeting at Chowpatty Beach [Bombay], the British Deputy Commissioner, whose job it was to put me under arrest, was visibly upset at having to do so. When we got into the car, he said: 'You bloody fool, Masani, why did you have to do this?' I understood that he wasn't being abusive, just a little affectionate and concerned that somebody with my background – because we had a very eminent father – had chosen to break the law and show such contempt for it. He was quite unhappy that he had to do his job.

Similarly, during the year I spent in Nasik Central Prison, in very good company of fifty or sixty 'politicals', none of us could ever complain of ill-treatment. When you went to the gaoler's office, you were told, 'Mr Masani, take your seat,' and there was a very civil conversation. There was never any attempt at humiliation, as might have happened in other countries. In fact, we bourgeois political leaders of the Congress Party were treated like officers and gentlemen during a war. It was accepted that we were nice chaps who were misled and had to be dealt with as such.

I do know that I was let out of prison on parole, as were other political prisoners, for a few days. Whenever there was illness in the family, or there was a particular reason for a prisoner to be out, he was given parole for eight days or fifteen days, at the end of which he, of course, took care to return in time to the prison. He was trusted on his own parole; and there was no attempt at surveillance. There was that relationship on both sides – in other words, we played cricket.

Imprisonment on these terms was not that different from being at some particularly strict Anglo-Indian boarding school; and it produced its own crop of good-natured pranks and escapades. The poet, Harindranath Chattopadhyaya, who wanted privacy to work while he was in prison, describes how he got a cell to himself by inciting fellow-inmates to sing revolutionary songs.

I was put along with ninety prisoners in a big cell, and I wanted to get out of the place. I was the author of a Hindi song, which went:
'The battle has begun, the battle has begun,
Men and women, side by side, will fight it.
You may flourish your *lathis*, you may do what you like,
But our blood is not cold, it is a wave of fire.'

It was a strong song, and it became very popular among the younger people; and we would sing it together. I was sent for by the Superintendant, who was a Britisher. He said: 'I'm sorry, your voice is very loud, and you are leading a revolution inside the prison. What do you mean by singing that song?' I said: 'That's my song, and it's very well known, and I see no harm at all in my friends singing it,' he said. 'Go back and don't let this happen again.' I laughed.

The next time we sang it, this man came along and said: 'You're to go to the Superintendant, and now you're going to be given a very stern punishment.' 'All right', I said; and I went. He said: 'Again you have done the same thing, and I asked you not to do it. I'm going to give you solitary confinement.' I liked the idea, and I said: 'Indeed, that's wonderful, I wish you would, because I am really tired of big crowds, so do put me in a solitary cell.'

He complied with my request. After I went to the cell, the Superintendant came to see me and asked: 'Could I get you some eggs, some good breakfast? I feel that you're used to a better life than most people here.' I said: 'No, I'm sorry, you can't do that, I'm not going to accept it. But I'm a writer, and I'd like my paper and pen. That's all that I need.' He gave it to me and said: 'I hope you'll be comfortable.' He was a very warm-hearted, very good man, and I liked him very much. He was a *pukka* gentleman, a really good Englishman.

Such gentlemanly banter between British gaolers and westernised nationalists was a familiar feature of the struggle for independence; but it was not the whole story. As M. R. Masani reminds us, the treatment of prisoners varied considerably from one province to another, and even within the same jail, depending on how they were classified.

It would be wrong to generalise from my pleasant experience, because there were prisoners in the north, for instance, who complained of very brutal and humiliating treatment. Even in the Bombay Presidency,[1] the 'C' class prisoners – volunteers who came from the lower orders of society – were certainly not treated with the same consideration. So there was discrimination according to education and your class.

The only instance of ill-treatment I experienced personally was in the north. I'd gone to Punjab as Secretary of the Congress Socialist Party, and I'd broken the law asking me to leave the province. I

1 The old British Indian province of Bombay.

waited for the police to come, and when they came to arrest me they produced handcuffs and suggested I put my wrists into them. I flatly declined, on the ground that I'd waited for them to come and arrest me, so the question of my running away did not arise. They maintained that in the north political prisoners did run away, so it was necessary. I said I wasn't one of them. When I threatened to have a little sparring with them, they gave up and agreed not to handcuff me. . . . I would say the Punjab police traditionally are pretty brutal.

Aruna Asaf Ali, who also experienced imprisonment as one of the privileged category, says she found the glaring discrimination between 'A' and 'C' class prisoners an insulting form of divide-and-rule tactics, designed to sow discord in nationalist ranks. But the Raj justified such discrimination on the ground that prisoners ranged across the political spectrum, from non-violent Gandhians to terrorist extremists.

It was certainly true that Indian nationalism was never just a family revolt by anglicised Indians who had come of age. Within Congress and outside, there were always other, more strident, voices prophecying the extermination of all things British. They appealed partly to Hindu religious sentiment, but also to the frustration of thousands of young Indians who were emerging from the universities to find themselves unemployed. For them, the nationalist movement had the intensity of a war of independence; and they saw it as a war begun by the British at Jallianwallah Bagh in Amritsar in 1919, when troops opened fire on an unarmed crowd, killing about 400 people and wounding more than a thousand. Shiva Dua remembers that her student activism in the 1930s was rooted in childhood memories of that massacre.

We lived in an atmosphere that we were going to fight a war with the British government, which was an alien government. I was very, very small when I heard this, about five. When the Jallianwallah Bagh tragedy took place, and the National Congress session took place in 1919, I remember having gone there as a child, along with a large number of volunteers from the school where my sister was principal. The girls sang a very important song which said: 'We will never be vanquished, even if we have to lay down our lives for the sake of the country.' Then we were taken to the Jallianwallah Bagh, and I was literally picked up and shown the bullet-marks in the walls. We brought blood-stained, red earth back from Jallianwallah Bagh, and my sister said: 'This is a sacred thing. It has to be kept in a silver casket. And every day it will be your duty to put flowers on it. Early in the morning, this will be your first duty to do.'

Soon after that there was a sort of fair, with toys and all kinds of things. My father gave me some money and said: 'Go and buy anything you like.' I went round and came back and said: 'I want this book.' It was called *The Punjab Massacre*, a small book in Hindi about Jallianwallah Bagh. He didn't want me to buy it, because I was five at that time, and he said: 'What will you do with this book?' I said: 'I want to read it.' It cost only eight annas,[1] and I bought it. At the age of five, I went through that book, not once, but many times.

Gandhi tried to channel such nationalist fervour into non-violent protest and into what he called 'constructive work' – his campaigns for *Swadeshi* and against untouchability. But there were several revolutionary secret societies which scorned his moderation and believed in armed struggle. Bengal was the traditional hotbed of revolutionary activity, as Tara Ali Baig, who grew up in the midst of it, explains.

> Just as the British love ghosts and haunted houses, the Bengalis like to do things surreptitiously. They love something that is secret and between each other and a kind of plot. . . . The fight against the British took this form of terrorism in Bengal because there were a very large number of highly educated young people who were very frustrated because there were absolutely no job opportunities for them. The only thing for an educated young man in those days was to go into the police, the ICS or the law. There was practically no other outlet. So there was a great deal of frustration among educated young men and women who felt that it was only when we were independent that they would be able to have a life and that the only way to do it was by terrorism.

Jatin Chakrabarti, now a minister in the Left Front Government of West Bengal, was a typical young sympathiser of the revolutionary societies as a student in the late 1920s. He confesses that their exploits had much of the drama and suspense of a contemporary thriller serial.

> That spirit of adventure, usually engrained in young people, was one of the reasons for the attraction. . . . We used to read the revolutionary literature proscribed by the Government. One of the best littérateurs in Bengali, S. Chatterji, wrote a book in which the hero was being hounded by the British police and could take different guises to avoid arrest. His organisation was very secret, and this secretiveness appealed to us.

In real life, too, there were revolutionary heroes renowned for their glamorous escapes, like Virendranath Chattopadhyaya, brother of the poet, Harindranath.

> He was very much a wanted man, there was £10,000 offered for his head at one time. He was considered to be a very important revolutionary. But they couldn't get him, because my brother was a tremendous linguist – he knew sixteen languages and spoke them fluently – and he was wonderful at make-up, changing his face. At every corner he was hunted by the police, but by the time he got to the next place he was different, speaking Arabic or some other language he knew. So he baffled the police, and they never got him.

1 In British Indian currency, sixteen annas made one rupee, the equivalent of two shillings.

Equally important to the revolutionary legend was the martyrdom of those whom the police did capture, leaders like Jatin Das, who died in prison after a sixty-three-day hunger strike. C. Sehanabish had just arrived in Calcutta as a student at the time, fresh from the humdrum monotony of life in a small district town. He describes how he was swept up in a vast tide of nationalist lamentation.

> 1929 was a thrilling year for me. I was reading every day in the papers about the hunger strike of the Lahore Conspiracy Case prisoners. My cousin Ajoy Kumar Ghosh, who later became General Secretary of the Communist Party of India, was among them, and of course Bhagat Singh too. And on the sixty-third day came the fateful news that Jatin Das was dead and that his body was being brought to Calcutta from Lahore, quite a distance. His body came in a coffin. I was at Howrah station waiting for the train to come, and there were lakhs of people waiting. Not knowing too many people, I kept asking eagerly: 'Who is that leader? Who is she?' – they were all there at the station. From there we took the body to Howrah Municipal Hall, where it was kept, and the next day we took out a procession which was the longest I had ever seen till then.

The revolutionaries drew their inspiration, not from British liberalism, but from Irish nationalism and the Easter Rebellion of 1916. Sehanabish remembers how impressed they were by the martyrdom of Sinn Fein leaders like Terence MacSwiney, who also died in prison on hunger strike.

> It was widely reported in our papers about this Irish revolt of 18th April – that Ireland, so near England, almost a stone's throw, but even then they could retain power. The hunger strike was a peculiar weapon used by both Irish and Bengali revolutionaries. Maybe we were influenced by them. MacSwiney died after 72 days of hunger-strike; and when Jatin Das died here after 63 days, one of the things I remember was the telegram from Mrs Mary MacSwiney, wife of the great leader: 'Ireland joins India in grief and pride over the death of Jatin Das. Freedom shall come.'

The nearest that the Bengali revolutionaries got to an armed uprising of their own was in the Chittagong Armoury Raid, launched symbolically on 18 April 1930, the anniversary of the Irish Revolt. A well-organised group of raiders, which included two women, captured the British armouries in Chittagong, took over the town and proclaimed a liberated zone. Although they were evicted after a pitched battle with government troops, they carried on a guerrilla campaign which lasted almost four years. Many Indians, including some who disapproved of their methods, admired such courage; but in the eyes of the Raj, the revolutionaries remained mere terrorists and were treated accordingly. Some were sentenced and hanged, some tortured to death, and others shot in alleged escape attempts. Jatin Chakrabarti describes the police methods that became routine in dealing with them.

To extort confessions from them, in the Special Branch of the police, they were subjected to various methods of third-degree. They were tortured like anything; powerful lights were focused on them; then pins were thrust under their finger-nails. Sometimes they were made to sleep on a slab of ice; sometimes they were made to lie on a bed and, from the top, drops of cold water used to fall on their foreheads, it was adjusted in such a way. Apart from that, there was very severe beating. They were wrapped up in blankets, and many constables were asked to beat them mercilessly with batons.

British police officers rarely soiled their own hands with this sort of interrogation; it was delegated to Indian subordinates. But Jatin Chakrabarti still remembers a British Police Commissioner, Sir Charles Taggart, who directed anti-terrorist operations in Calcutta and survived several assassination attempts.

He was very, very notorious, and went out of his way to try out methods of torture on the revolutionaries. He was very efficient, and it was reputed that he was trained at Scotland Yard and specially deputed for repressing the revolutionary movement. As a result, three attempts were made on his life; but unfortunately for us, every time he escaped. Dalhousie Square has now been dedicated to the memory of the martyrs who died in an attempt to kill him. They stormed the Writer's Building[1] and entered the chamber of the Inspector-General of Police, who was scheduled to have a meeting with Taggart; but Taggart was fortunate enough to come a little late. At the appointed hour, they stormed the building and killed the Inspector-General; and Taggart, because he came late, was saved.

In several districts of Bengal, assassination was a danger that British officials had to live with, especially if they had a reputation for ill-treating nationalists. Yet, even at its worst, says Tara Ali Baig, this did not disrupt normal social life in the province.

Looking at terrorism today, I can't help feeling that was a rather polite kind of terrorism. There was no question of bombing groups of innocent people. There were definitely targeted individuals; or else it was like an armoury raid to collect ammunition and guns. Every official had to carry a revolver; it was mandatory. But they were awfully careless about it, because it really didn't seem to matter very much if they had one or not. At our dinner-parties, there was always a table set aside where the revolvers used to be put systematically before dinner and collected after dinner. But almost invariably, the next day, we found some under the cushions or somewhere else, and somebody had forgotten their self-protection.

Not all British officers were terrorist targets or terrorist hunters. Tara

1 The Bengal provincial Secretariat building in Calcutta.

Ali Baig describes how an unusual British district officer she knew tried to bridge the political chasm.

> He asked me to drop in and have breakfast. When I went there, he took me straight into his study. There were two young men sitting there; and very prominently, his revolver was sitting on the desk. He said in a very conversational voice: 'I wanted you to meet these young men, Tara, because they are in jail for terrorism.' We had a very nice chat; and they were nice, very well brought up, young men. I'm sure he left his revolver there on purpose, because what he wanted to establish was the fact that there was really nothing to fear, because there was trust between them.

By the 1940s, the Raj was finding it increasingly difficult to separate the revolutionary wolves from the Gandhian sheep where nationalists were concerned. Most revolutionary groups had by then merged into the left wing of Congress under the charismatic banner of the Bengali leader, Subhas Chandra Bose, who was President of Congress from 1938 to 1939. Bose had close links with the revolutionary secret societies and rejected non-violence. Unlike Gandhi and his heir-apparent, Jawaharlal Nehru, he stood for an all-out confrontation with the Raj, including an alliance with the Axis powers in the Second World War on the principle that 'my enemy's enemies are my friends'. Harindranath Chatto- padhyaya, who knew both Nehru and Bose intimately, sums up the difference between them.

> Nehru and Subhas were diametrically opposed to each other in their whole attitude towards the country and its freedom. Jawahar- lal was essentially a kind of Englishman, and a very fine Englishman. . . . Subhas Bose was a Bengali who could die on the gallows if he fell in love with a woman; but he fell in love with India, and he could die for India. When he was in college, the Principal, an Englishman, said something to him about India. He caught hold of the Principal by the scruff of his neck, dragged him down a staircase and threw him down. That was his temperament – he came to boiling point when it came to India.

When Bose failed to break the hold of Gandhi and Nehru over Congress, he chose to escape into exile and join the Japanese in their advance on India. Yet, it was his example, more than Gandhi's, that inspired the Quit India movement, launched in August 1942, after the British had refused to consider any form of responsible government for the duration of the war. The August Revolt, as it was known, aimed to make India ungovernable; and with the arrest of the senior Congress leaders, it was led by an underground group of young radicals. Aruna Asaf Ali, whose beauty and oratory made her its romantic heroine, remembers it as the most exciting period of her life.

> Although Nehru was the predominant influence in my life, Subhas Bose's escape and his broadcasts calling for armed struggle struck a bell. Similarly, we heard about the partisans in occupied Europe,

the French partisans and other stories. This underground idea for me was really fighting a partisan war. In those days one was very romantic. . . . That period was thrilling – just managing to get out of the clutches of the police, half an hour after you've left you'd hear that they've raided the place. Those were moments when you just somehow managed to get into a car, and someone mysteriously led you to another house. You didn't know where you were going and spending nights.

Rejecting the traditional Gandhian method of courting arrest, the underground activists did their best to stay out of prison. For Mrs Asaf Ali, this involved some narrow escapes.

I'd just gone to a place in Bihar and thought it was far too secluded for anyone to know I was there. I managed to get a nice little place done up to stay there, because I was very sick physically and wanted a little rest. I was just about settled, when suddenly a person motored down from Calcutta to say: 'Leave this place immediately. The police have already arrived at the station and they're on their way here.' He had a rickety old car, and we got into it. That drive I'll never forget – rushing away like mad, knowing that they were already perhaps chasing us, almost like a film chase. Suddenly, we found a deserted temple, where I managed to hide. This fellow went away with the car; after he went round and saw that all was clear, he came back for me late in the evening. Then he took me to Asansol station to catch a train for Bombay. At night nobody would open their compartments; only one third-class compartment was open, and I just jumped into that and found somewhere to sit. They had all been asleep and were very irritated. 'Who is this woman?' they were muttering away among themselves.

Another time, I had managed to stay at an Anglo-Indian boarding-house in Calcutta. The landlady didn't know who I was and asked me: 'Where is your husband?' My husband had been arrested; so I tried to keep as near as possible to the truth and said: 'My husband is a prisoner of war.' Then she was all sympathy for me. But one afternoon we were having tea, and in walked an Englishman, a friend of hers. I was startled beyond words. I didn't know whether he was from the police and whether somebody had told him I was there. I think I did a very good piece of acting, looking back on it, and just made polite conversation. He turned out to be an Englishman who was passing through Calcutta and was not a part of the establishment. He asked me: 'What do you think of the Movement?' Again, trying to be very truthful, I said: 'I think it's a marvellous thing that's happened. We Indians have at last got to know who we are and how we have been exploited by you people.' After I had finished my story about why some of us were thinking of joining the Movement, he said: 'Well, if I were you, I would probably have done the same.' And he left. That was some relief, because apart from my being arrested, what used to worry me was that people like the landlady had unknowingly given me shelter, and what business had I to involve them in anything that would jeopardise their careers?

While Mrs Asaf Ali led a charmed existence, always one step ahead of the police, many of her followers were less fortunate. Khushwant Singh, whose father remained an ardent loyalist, remembers how his brother's links with the underground threw his family into crisis.

Mrs Asaf Ali came to see me one night, wearing a *burkha*,[1] and asked whether I could help her to buy a duplicator. I said that I disapproved of the Movement, because I thought it was necessary to fight the fascists and not the British at that time. But I mentioned it to my brother, who was foolish enough to go and buy a duplicator, not realising that the name of the buyer had to be recorded. He handed it to Mrs Asaf Ali; and later the duplicator was taken in some raid by the police, and they tracked it down to my brother, who was taken for questioning to the police station. My father was absolutely aghast, because he was expecting a knighthood that year, and he thought this had finished his career forever. Sir Evan Jenkins was the Chief Commissioner of Delhi, and my father went and saw him. Sir Evan was very understanding: my brother was released after a while, my father got his knighthood, and nothing happened.

It was a time when some of the most loyal and illustrious families in the land faced similar rebellions by their nationalist offspring; and the British made allowances for such youthful exuberance among the upper classes. But thousands of activists from less privileged backgrounds had to face the kind of treatment previously reserved for alleged terrorists. Usha Mehta describes some of the methods used to clamp down on a clandestine radio station with which she was involved.

We started an underground radio and called it Congress Radio. I remember the announcement that we used to make: 'This is Congress Radio speaking from somewhere in India on 42.34 metres.' Our radio gave the people all the news about the Movement, which the Congress Party used to collect from different corners of the country; and some of the leaders used to deliver speeches and give messages to the people to carry on the Movement. The Government was terribly disturbed about this, and they tried to chase us and also to harass us. They arrested most of the radio dealers, and even the employees were not only arrested but harassed so much that they were made to sleep on ice-slabs and kept in isolated cells. I myself had to stay in an isolated cell for about six months in a jail in Bombay.

Congress demonstrators had by now grown accustomed to police *lathi*-charges. But the Quit India movement, with its attempts at

1 The traditional black, hooded cloak worn by veiled Muslim women.

sabotaging the war effort, was met by new levels of police violence which are still widely remembered. Wounded demonstrators, left lying unattended in the streets, became a familiar sight; and citizens' relief units were organised on a voluntary basis to provide medical aid to the injured. According to Usha Mehta, women volunteers joined the Movement in large numbers and bore some of the worst casualties.

> The police were absolutely brutal in their attitude towards women, and even pregnant women were not spared. Women were victims of brutal *lathi*-charges. Not only were they insulted and abused, but many of them were even raped. One of them in Bombay, I know, was raped not by one officer but by officer after officer, including the British officers. She was a worker in one of the mills. She found it extremely difficult to return home, and she wanted to commit suicide. It was only with great difficulty that some of the Congress women could persuade her not to do that and take her home.

At a time when India was a crucial wartime base for the British, neither non-violent demonstrations nor sporadic sabotage stood any real chance of overthrowing the Raj; but they provoked the authorities into a widespread use of repression which severely undermined the moral basis of British rule and of the war effort itself. Indians, it seemed, were being asked to sacrifice their lives in an ostensibly anti-fascist war, while being denied basic civil liberties in their own country. The Quit India movement served to demonstrate that the intransigence of the Raj had united nationalists of very different political hues – non-violent Gandhians and revolutionary terrorists, anti-fascist socialists and religious revivalists – in a sense of moral outrage which preferred anarchy, or even Japanese occupation, to British rule. For M. R. Masani, an LSE-bred anti-fascist, the moment of reckoning came while he was evading arrest along with one of the underground leaders, Achyut Patwardhan.

> We were wanted by the police; and we were in a taxi in Bombay going from one place to another. 'Achyut,' I asked, 'when independence comes, will it all be very beautiful? I have my doubts.' 'Of course, it won't,' he replied. But we both agreed that, since good government was no substitute for self-government, it was worth throwing the British out, even if what followed wasn't very agreeable.

IMPERIAL RETREAT

If British empire-builders could have kept racialism out of their
policy, I'm sure that they could happily have stayed on in India to
this day. That racial discrimination was absolutely blatant as and
when Indian fighting forces came in contact with the British
fighting forces. If an Indian had any kind of self-respect, he couldn't
help resenting it. Even today, after so many years, I hesitate to go to
any white man's country. During that impressionable period of my
life, the treatment I got from Britishers, from white people, was so
bad that even today I fear I might meet the same thing.

B. C. Dutt (ex-rating in the Royal Indian Navy and a leader of the Mutiny of 1946)

The Quit India movement coincided with an event which did more than
any police repression to shake Indian confidence in the Raj and blacken
its memory. This was the cataclysmic Bengal famine of 1943, which
claimed, at a conservative estimate, some three million lives. Both Indian
nationalists and the colonial rulers agreed that it was an artificial, man-
made scarcity; but while the Government attributed it to panic-buying
and hoarding, most Indians blamed the callous neglect of an administration preoccupied with the British war effort. Ashok Mitra, an economist
who later served as West Bengal's Finance Minister, gives a relatively
dispassionate account of what happened:

> That was a year when production in Bengal was slightly above
> normal. But the British were worried about Japanese infiltration –
> they were right next to our border in Burma – and they didn't allow
> or encourage any movement from the surplus districts to the deficit
> districts. They withdrew all the boats; and during the war there was
> rationing of petrol, so that even trucks and lorries could not move.
> In any case, licences were issued by the administration. Therefore,
> although the grain was there, there was no trading in grain. The
> deficit areas were starved of grain, and people died.

The war contributed to the famine in several ways. Supplies of
Burmese rice were cut off by the Japanese occupation; local pressure on
food supplies was increased by the presence in Bengal of large numbers of
Allied troops; and the grain merchants decided to maximise their
wartime profits by hoarding existing stocks. Most important of all, trade
in Bengal, which relied heavily on river transport, was crippled by the
Government's policy of 'boat denial', the scuttling and confiscation of
private boats to prevent them falling into the hands of the advancing
Japanese.

Nevertheless, some of those who attempted to organise voluntary relief aid at the time say that all these difficulties could have been overcome if the authorities had shown the necessary political will. Renuka Ray, then a member of the Central Legislative Assembly and active in the relief campaign, still believes that there was a conspiracy of silence which extended from the provincial administration in Bengal up to the War Cabinet in London. Britain's reluctance, she says, to admit the gravity of the famine induced Churchill to reject American offers of grain, while the authorities in India made no effort to rush emergency supplies to Bengal from other parts of the country. The availability of boats was restricted long after the Japanese threat had receded; and even supplies raised by voluntary donations were at first refused access to East Bengal, the area worst affected, on the ground that they would cause panic.

> When I heard about the famine conditions, I came to Calcutta and then went to East Bengal, where it was very bad. After seeing all this, I went back to Delhi, and we were able to send a number of railway wagons full of foodstuffs, which were donated by the public and by various business firms. After we had sent them, I heard that they were stuck in Calcutta and not allowed to go to East Bengal. So I rushed back and met Mr Suhrawardy,[1] who was then in charge of Food and Civil Supplies. He was very callous and indifferent and said: 'Mrs Ray, this famine is a man-made one, and you people are creating it. There is no famine.' They were saying that we were creating panic; and I think Suhrawardy himself had been taken in by that propaganda. Afterwards he changed his mind, because it became so bad that thousands upon thousands started coming up to Calcutta from the districts, asking for food and dying in front of them. The cry was 'Give Us Food!' – nobody wanted money or anything else. I had a lot of trouble sending those wagons to the districts; but we did eventually with the help of Sir J. P. Srivastava, the Food Member of the Viceroy's Cabinet.

At a time when Indian opinion was already incensed at being plunged into a British war without any consultation, the Bengal famine seemed to offer gruesome evidence that the Raj regarded Indians as mere fodder for its military machine; and Indian loyalty to empire reached its lowest ebb at the very moment when Britain most desperately required it. Many relatively non-political Indians remember tuning in enthusiastically to Japanese and German wartime broadcasts and rejoicing over British defeats. By 1942, such disloyalty was seriously affecting morale among the forces of law and order themselves. K. F. Rustamji, the present Chairman of the Indian Government's Police Commission, was then an up-and-coming young police officer. He says that most Indian officers of his generation, though loyal to their professional duties, were also nationalists of some sort. This conflict of loyalties, he says, divided him from his British colleagues when he had to deal with nationalist protest during the Quit India movement.

[1] Bengal's leading Muslim politician, who later served as Prime Minister of Pakistan.

I was posted as City Superintendent of Nagpur. It was easy to deal with the crowds; but I found it very difficult to deal with some young officers who felt it was their duty to suppress the people by firing. Quite distinct from any orders that were given by me or by senior officers, they'd pick up a 303 rifle and fire at a crowd half a mile away; they'd fire at a window if some woman had thrown a stone. That type of thing was very difficult to deal with, because I was an Indian and they were not.

I came from a family which was intensely nationalistic. My brother was a lawyer; and in 1942, while I was dealing with the riots, my brother was inciting them. He was a professor in the Law College, and he was behind a large amount of the student agitation that occurred in Nagpur. All the time my family was telling me to get out of the police force, and yet I was not sure. There was a conflict in my mind, as there must have been in the mind of every Indian at that time, whether to support the British or throw them out.

Almost every day, there was something or other that you disagreed with, and you felt you had to take a different line. In the end, I had a big row with them, because they wanted me to keep several people who were sick and injured in custody. I went against that order and released them on bail. After that, we had several conflicts, and they felt that perhaps it would be best to move me. So I was moved out of Nagpur and then rewarded with a medal for having saved the city from a great deal of damage.

Even more worrying for the Raj than disaffection in its police force was the intense nationalism of younger Indian army officers. Many who remained loyal to their regiments nevertheless felt a sneaking admiration for the Indian National Army or INA, set up behind Japanese lines by Subhas Bose. Some prisoners-of-war from the British Indian army actually went over to the other side. The British called them traitors and deserters and claimed that the Japanese had bought them over with special privileges. But Brigadier Tony Bhagat, who served in both the British Indian Army and the INA, vehemently denies that people like him were taking the soft option.

If the Japanese lost the war, the chances were that people who joined the Indian National Army would be dealt with very harshly, even shot as deserters; so there was a great risk attached to it. On the other hand, officers who didn't join the INA could remain prisoners-of-war, and, being Indians, were treated much better than other prisoners-of-war. On the conclusion of the war, they could go back to India and find their old places in the Indian Army, as happened. There was also propaganda to the effect that officers who joined the Indian National Army lived in a grand way, had plenty of money and enjoyed themselves. This was not correct. We were given the same pay as the prisoner-of-war officers. No doubt, we had better accommodation, because we had to function from there in training the troops. But otherwise, we were in no way better off, nor did we have a very enjoyable time.

The British Indian army was a mercenary army. The officers and *jawans* were serving in it in order to get a good salary and have a good life. The Indian National Army had only one object, and that was to secure the freedom of their country. They did not have very good pay; there was no question of rewards after the war. They were trained in the normal way; but nationalist fervour was encouraged by songs about the Motherland and about the exploits of our leaders; and there were dramas and things like that with the object of inculcating a nationalist spirit. The number of Indian commissioned officers was very limited, and therefore a large number of senior non-commissioned officers were promoted as officers of the INA. Naturally, these officers, who came from the rank and file, mixed a great deal with the soldiers.

According to Bhagat, the loyalty of INA officers was not to the Japanese but to Indian independence, and his own refusal to toe the Japanese line landed him back in detention.

I was most anxious that we did not force the British to leave India and at the same time put the Japanese in their place. I was anxious that the Japanese government in Tokyo should very clearly lay down their war aims as far as India was concerned. This they were most reluctant to do. You could get all these assurances from their local commanders in Malaya, but they were not forthcoming from the Prime Minister of Japan. I had an opportunity to talk to Bose, and I made clear my reservations on this point.

Since the Japanese never really gave the INA a chance to prove its military mettle, its main impact remained political. When the Japanese retreated from south-east Asia, INA troops surrendered to the British. They were brought back to India and held in the Red Fort at Delhi, where the mutineers of 1857 had made their last stand. Their trial for treason, far from discrediting them, became their finest hour, drawing far wider nationalist publicity and sympathy than they had commanded in action. B. C. Dutt, then a rating in the Royal Indian Navy, describes how the INA's example affected him and other young Indian servicemen.

The whole country was aroused in such a way that it penetrated the barrack walls. It reached us, and we knew all about it. For the first time, many of us started feeling: 'What have we been fighting for – the preservation of empire? Shouldn't our own country be free?' And many of us started feeling guilty for being in uniform.

Ratings of the Royal Indian Navy had fought side by side with British and white Commonwealth troops in the combined operation, led by Lord Mountbatten, to drive the Japanese out of Burma. But racial discrimination had prevented any real comradeship in arms; and according to B. C. Dutt, Indian seamen had returned from the Burma campaign with a deep sense of resentment.[1]

The war and naval discipline had cut off the ratings from political events; and few had more than an inkling of what had been happening in the country at large during the Quit India movement. But by 1945, the end of the war and the prospect of demobilisation and unemployment were giving a new edge to old grievances about service conditions. The nucleus of disaffection was a shore establishment in Bombay called *HMS Talwar*. It was the headquarters of the communications ratings, who tended to be better educated and more politically conscious than their fellow seamen. B. C. Dutt, who became their leader, tells the story of how a relatively minor act of protest in January 1946 snowballed into an armed revolt that shook the military foundations of the Raj.

> Our group started staging little demonstrations to arouse the other ratings. In one of those subversive activities, I was arrested; and my arrest opened the eyes of many. I became a hero among the boys. . . . The occasion I was arrested was the first time that the Commander-in-Chief was coming to visit *HMS Talwar*, and everything was made spick and span. He was to take the salute from a platform, and a march past was to take place. The night before, we managed to write 'Quit India' on the walls and the platform from which he was to take the salute. A lot of effort went into doing that; the authorities felt that something might happen, so lots of guards were kept and floodlights were kept on all the time. In spite of that, we managed it; and I also managed to distribute a lot of anti-British leaflets. But then, in the morning, I was caught, and they kept me in the lock-up until the Commander-in-Chief's visit was over. Then, of course, I had to face the music. I was kept in solitary confinement for fifteen days because they couldn't decide what to do with me – whether to make me another INA-type hero or quietly hush up the whole thing. Finally, they decided to hush it up, and I was released. I was to be sacked from the navy; but the order to sack me took 48 hours to come through, and for those 48 hours they left me in the barracks. That was a big mistake on the part of the commanding officer, who didn't realise what was happening in the navy, didn't have a clue. I had two clear days to work, and by then I had become a hero to every rating in *HMS Talwar*.
>
> We had an all-night meeting. There was no guard, because the war had ended and there was not so much discipline; and the officers anyway couldn't care less, because their future was almost as uncertain as ours. That first night, we couldn't decide what to do. But we knew that something had to be done which would be collective, so that it would appear as a mutiny and the authority would be thrown out.
>
> The second night, when we met, somebody suggested: 'Let us

1 See pages 30–31.

refuse to eat breakfast. If all of us refuse to eat breakfast, that will be mutiny; and once the mutiny happens, we'll take over the navy. Once we take over the navy, those national leaders who have gone underground to fight the British will come and lead us.'

So the next day, when we went to the breakfast-table, somebody said: 'The food is rotten! We won't eat it!' We all came out of the barracks; we were about 1500 ratings in *Talwar* in those days. The Indian officers didn't know what to do; and one or two British officers who were there got so scared, seeing for the first time all the ratings refuse to do something together, they didn't do anything. We had complete freedom, and we just went berserk. We could now talk openly, clearly, loudly for anybody to hear. And we said: 'Our situation, our future, our country's future are never going to be what we want them to be, so long as the British are here. The British must go! That is our slogan.' The next day, we managed to get the other important barrack, Castle Barrack, where the seamen ratings were, with us. And by evening all the establishments in Bombay had thrown their officers out. We approached the Bombay papers, and by the next morning the news was all around the world, and the mutiny had started.

Within 48 hours, the revolt had spread by wireless contact across the entire Indian Navy, at sea and ashore. It was led by a committee which included Hindus, Muslims and Sikhs and maintained throughout a communal unity which was unique in the prevailing climate of sectarian hostility and Muslim separatism. The mutineers appealed to both the Congress and the Muslim League[1] to join in leading them.

In our innocent minds, we thought: 'The people outside are fighting for the country's cause. The national leaders will come and give us the lead.' That was our first mistake. None of us had any clue about the political world outside the barrack-rooms. We only knew that our national leaders were keen to get the British out and make the country free, and we thought we were contributing to that.

But the tradition of non-violent and constitutional politics proved too strong for the leaders of either of the two major parties even to consider joining the mutiny. The politicians took fright at the prospect of an armed insurrection which might jeopardise the bargains they were busy striking at the negotiating table; and they joined instead in a call to the ratings to surrender. Though abandoned by the politicians, the mutineers received unexpected support from Bombay mill-workers, who threw up barricades in the city's industrial areas and fought pitched battles with British troops. According to B. C. Dutt, it was a largely spontaneous, mass uprising.

For the first time in Bombay city, the British had to bring in tanks to put down the workers. It was the individual workers, who knew

1 The main Muslim party, which was by then demanding a separate, Muslim state of Pakistan.

that the ratings were trying to do something great for the country, particularly when they heard that water had been cut off to *Talwar* and Castle Barracks and that we were being starved into surrender. That infuriated them. This was the first time that the workers saw their boys in uniform, instead of fighting for the empire, fighting for their country at long last; and they were going to be starved into surrender. They all rose, irrespective of political parties. In some parts of Bombay, they literally dug up roads and put up a fight against tanks with stones. That is how more than 350 people died and more than a thousand were injured.

At first it looked as though the trouble might spread to disaffected army and air force units, where similar rumblings of discontent had been heard. But the Government acted swiftly to pre-empt a repetition of 1857, rushing in reinforcements from the Royal Navy and Air Force and from British army regiments. Encircled by overwhelmingly superior numbers, and starved of both supplies and political support, the mutineers hoisted the white flag four days after it all began. B. C. Dutt still maintains – and there are historians who agree with him – that, if the politicians had backed the ratings, India might have achieved independence without partition.

There would have been bloodshed, certainly; but it would have been much less than what happened when the British left India. The massacres in Punjab and Bengal would have been avoided. Our struggle was gradually affecting the Indian army, which would have risen also, at least part of it; and certainly the major part of the Royal Indian Air Force would have been with us. There would have been a fight; many of us would have died, but there would have been far less bloodshed than in 1947.

As it was, the abortive mutiny certainly hastened a negotiated transfer of power and strengthened the bargaining position of the very politicians who had disowned it. The mutineers, although they did not know it at the time, had scored an important point. By demonstrating that the Raj could no longer count on the loyalty of Indian troops, they finally convinced British policy-makers that it was time to quit India, and quickly. The Raj had always recognised that India had been won and held ultimately by the sword; but post-war Britain could not afford the military price that this would involve without loyal Indians to do the job.

The imperial retreat, once decided, took place with what many Indians regarded as unseemly haste and a callous disregard for its consequences. There were British officers who worked conscientiously till the last day; but many others sat back and gloated while Hindus and Muslims fought an undeclared civil war. Especially in Punjab, where the carnage was worst, there remains a strong suspicion that the British did the minimum to stop it, for reasons that Khushwant Singh explains.

Their real attitude was: 'You stew in your own juice. You didn't want us; now you look after yourselves.' There was a certain amount of malicious pleasure in seeing that we were at each other's throats. They said: 'We told you that you can't run your own country; see what's happening.' So they kept aloof; and there was hardly any Englishman who took any interest in what was going on, apart from sending reports to the headquarters on what was happening. No one stuck his neck out.

The administration was also paralysed by the sudden withdrawal of many of its experienced officers. According to Rajeshwar Dayal, a senior Indian member of the ICS who was then Home Secretary of the United Provinces, most of his British colleagues preferred to take a golden handshake, rather than serve under Indian ministers.

They wondered if the country would really be able to manage on its own without their help. They left a lot of very important posts vacant when they left *en masse*, and we had to fill them all and assume the responsibilities which our British colleagues had just abandoned. Many of them just threw in their hats. They felt that there was no place for them in the future India. I think it was somewhat unjustified, because the Congress governments that came in were quite generous in their attitude to British officers who were sympathetic to the people of the country. There were indeed some of them. I asked the Inspector-General of Police, Sir George Pierce, a very fine man, to stay on; and he did stay a year or two longer. But in my province, not more than half a dozen officers of the police and civil service stayed on; and after another year or two, they too left.

Congress and Muslim League politicians, eager to divide the long-awaited spoils of office, were by now reconciled to the political costs of partition. But there were nationalists who found it hard to celebrate such a pyrrhic victory, among them Mahatma Gandhi himself and leaders of the recent Quit India movement like Aruna Asaf Ali.

My feelings were very mixed, because right up to 1946 the Socialist Party, which I belonged to by then, was carrying on a tearing, raging campaign – 'No compromise, no Pakistan'. I must have addressed thousands of meetings in 1947, trying to tell the people that these talks that are going on with the Cabinet Mission,[1] if they are going to lead to Pakistan, that means the end of our dream of a united India; and Gandhiji was with us. That soured our feelings about the character of the freedom we had got. 'It's a transfer of power,' I used to say. 'It is not revolutionary transformation at all.'

Added to this was the communal frenzy, Hindu-Muslim killing. That was saddening, confusing, baffling; and we didn't know what had happened. Our anger again was against the British – they had divided us religion-wise, they were behind the Muslim League. We all felt that, but for the encouragement the Muslim League got from

1 Delegated by the British Cabinet to negotiate the terms of independence.

them, we would have had a civil war situation perhaps, but it would have ended in the unity of India. So one part of me said: 'No, we should have carried on another struggle. More suffering, more blood, what of it? Without that, you don't get freedom.'

Back in London, too, there was some dismay at the suddenness of it all, though from motives that were often more selfish. Romesh Thapar, who was in England when independence was announced, still chuckles over a British neighbour's reaction.

We had below us a couple who were the dancing champions in England at that time. When the transfer of power took place, this girl ran up to us weeping and said: 'What is going to happen to England now? India's become free! Can you believe it?'

While the transfer of power opened up dramatic new vistas of promotion for Indian officers who had served the Raj, it offered little recognition to nationalists who had fought the British in the INA or in the naval mutiny. Brigadier Bhagat explains how he and other INA officers were cheated of their due.

After the British left, the army was opened up to the INA officers rejoining; but the terms were not at all favourable. The INA officers who rejoined were to be given a new commission with an acting rank that was the same as they had held at the time of the British surrender at Singapore. For instance, I was a major in 1941. In 1950, when I rejoined, I was recommissioned as a second lieutenant with the acting rank of major. The reason for this was that the Indian Army officers did not want a large number of senior officers from the INA to rejoin and thereby affect their own chances of promotion and high appointments. The excuse was that the INA officers had been out of touch with the army for three or four years; but this applied also to the prisoner-of-war officers who got back their rightful rank according to seniority.

Pandit Jawaharlal Nehru[1] was sympathetic towards the INA – he personally acted as a defence lawyer for the three officers who were put on trial by the British. But he was obliged to let down the INA, because the senior officers of the Indian Army said that either they were right in serving the Indian Army, or the INA officers were right in fighting against the British. In the interests of discipline, morale and efficiency in the Indian Army, the Prime Minister had no option but to take the advice of the Indian Army officers, and the INA was not given a fair deal.

INA officers were at least offered re-entry, even if it meant demotion. For more than 2000 naval ratings who had been sacked and put in detention camps, the prospects were even more bleak, as B. C. Dutt recalls.

1 India's first Prime Minister and head of the Interim Government to which the British handed over power.

When independence came, most of us were starving. After we came out of detention, most of us could not find jobs. Job opportunities were then very few, and mostly under British control. We were the Untouchables. In fact, I was starving for the next three years, not more than one meal a day. So naturally, we felt that this independence had very little to do with us. It was their independence, not ours.

At that time, the Indian government had so many other problems on its hands. Punjab and Bengal had gone up in smoke, and there was a fantastic refugee problem. The government consisted of men who had never had anything to do with the fighting forces. They had been led by Mahatma Gandhi, a man of non-violence, and they didn't have any military experience whatsoever. They were guided and advised by people in uniform; and who were they? The senior army officers had been brought up and trained by the British. And they advised: 'The most important thing is discipline. If you take the INA or the naval ratings back, that will demoralise the existing army.' As it was, the country was not in a stable condition. So the Indian leadership could not afford to ignore what they thought was the sane advice of the professional brass.

Hardly had the dust settled on the British withdrawal than it was becoming clear that the structures which the British had built and preserved over two hundred years had found new guardians. As the Congress tricolour replaced the Union Jack and India's jaunty national anthem rang out the Raj, the new rulers were already announcing that theirs was not a revolution of institutions or attitudes.

THE NEW RAJ

*Foreign rule, in any case, is bad; and I've no regrets that I
participated in obtaining independence for India under Gandhi's
leadership. But British rule in India was not malign; it was not
needlessly cruel. Way back in the nineteenth century, people like
Mountstuart Elphinstone[1] have been on record as saying that the
purpose of British rule was to educate Indians to be able to rule
themselves and for the British to retire. That's a concept which you
don't expect from foreign rulers a century before it happens. When
freedom came, the British left us valuable legacies, which have
come in very useful to us in ruling ourselves to some purpose.*

M. R. Masani (former Leader of the Opposition in the Indian Parliament)

*How can a civilised and enlightened people like the British have
kept us so backward and divided? They tried to educate a certain
middle-class and allowed it all the facilities; but the basic reforms
they did not carry out. Our literacy rates were so poor, and our
technology has taken years to catch up with modern developments.
They took mean advantage of our religious differences to say: 'You
are not prepared for self-rule.' They needn't have left us to chaos, as
they did, and divided our country. That was the worst – the
partition of India. That was criminal: all the poisonous weeds have
grown on that; and our present separatist situation flows from that
final act of Hindu state, Muslim state.*

Mrs Aruna Asaf Ali (nationalist leader)

Every year India's Republic Day celebrations held in New Delhi on 26
January are followed by the military spectacle of Beating Retreat. As the
stately domes and colonnades which were once the canopy of the Raj
turn golden pink in the setting sun, the Indian Camel Corps, silhouetted
on the ramparts in its colonial white-and-red uniforms, sounds the Last
Post, and a military band strikes up one of Mahatma Gandhi's favourite
hymns, 'Abide With Me'.

Such ceremonial is a striking reminder of India's unexpectedly fond
farewell to empire. Those who remember the jubilant crowds that
greeted independence on 15 August 1947 say that the British were never
more popular than at the moment of their departure. No sooner had the
Raj announced that it was leaving than all was forgiven. Even at the

---

1 Perhaps the most outstanding of all British Indian administrators, Elphinstone served as
Governor of Bombay (1819–27) and inspired the founding by Indians of the famous
Elphinstone College, one of the earliest institutions of Western higher education, set up in
1827.

height of the partition riots, which raged through the year of independence, no British man or woman came to any harm from the murderous mobs that stalked the land.

India's nationalist leaders, who were stepping out of jail and into the palaces of empire, were especially eager to let bygones be bygones. With anarchy, civil war and secession looming large on the horizon, their main concern was to restore strong and stable government; and that inevitably meant a heavy reliance on the machinery of government that the British were leaving behind.

India's political inheritance was symbolised by New Delhi, its grand, new capital, built by the Raj in the years after the First World War. At the time, nationalist leaders had condemned the imperial folly of a regime which was spending such vast sums on the panoply of power; but as rulers, they soon discovered that pomp and ceremonial had their uses. The architects of New Delhi were British – Sir Edwin Lutyens and Sir Herbert Baker – and the thousands of artisans and labourers who built it were from nearby Rajasthan. Lutyens and Baker relied on Indian contractors, foremost among whom was the Sikh builder, Sir Sobha Singh. His son, Khushwant Singh, was only a child when he watched the new city spring up, almost magically, out of a wilderness overrun by wild animals.

My father moved into New Delhi as soon as the announcement of the transfer of the capital from Calcutta to Delhi was made, and he was one of the people who actually carried the foundation-stone laid by the King at Kingsway Camp to its present site, because that site was found unsuitable. I came here as a boy of six, when there was no New Delhi. We lived in a shack, a few builders' families. I remember a tiny, little train called the Imperial Delhi Railway bringing in stone and gravel, and thousands of workers hammering and chiselling away at the stone, and the roads appearing slowly. And I remember the first building in Connaught Circus[1] going up. Then suddenly, after the war was over, other buildings started going up rapidly, and the newly planted trees grew, and the city took shape.

It was an expansive, imperialist city, with no such things as fortifications to defend it. Lutyens had this vision of enormous avenues with water-tanks running alongside. . . . But even then, it's quite clear that they knew they were leaving, because one thing they quarrelled over was the relevant heights of the Viceregal Lodge and the Secretariats. Baker wanted the two buildings to be on exactly the same height, because he said: 'This country will inevitably become free and a democracy, and the ruler and his civil servants must be on the same level.' Lutyens, on the other hand, said: 'It's the Oriental tradition that the ruler should be on a slight elevation above his subjects.' They quarrelled so bitterly that they were not on speaking terms; and the entire matter was about whether the Viceregal Lodge should be eighteen inches higher. Lutyens lost the battle and became very embittered.

[1] The commercial centre of the city.

One thing that the architects did agree on was the need to incorporate into their designs ornamental embellishments like domes, wall-railings and sculptured animals which were copied from India's ancient Hindu and Muslim monuments. The result was a distinctive, Eastern baroque style known as Indo-Saracenic, which used the traditional red sandstone of the region. Historical continuity was to be further emphasised by linking the new capital with the neighbouring ruins of imperial citadels built by former Hindu and Muslim dynasties. But Khushwant Singh says that a self-willed British vicereine drove a coach and horses through this idea.

> Lutyens' main design was very clear. He was going to build the Viceregal Lodge on top of the hill, and they were going to have one straight drive from it to the Purana Quila,[1] without any interruption, and another one at right angles going right up to the royal mosque, the Jama Masjid.[2] He was going to dam the River Jumna behind Humayun's tomb[3] to build a large riverside drive with a lake. All those plans had to be pruned because of the expense involved, and because a very headstrong vicereine who followed, Lady Willingdon, had the Willingdon Stadium built right in the middle, obstructing the view from Viceregal Lodge to Purana Quila.

The stately Viceregal Lodge, more irreverently described as a British matron in fancy dress, remains the crowning glory of what is called Lutyens Delhi. It is now the presidential palace of the Indian Republic; but its imperial etiquette lives on, thanks to the Sandhurst training of independent India's first Chief of Protocol, Rashid Ali Baig. His widow, Tara Ali Baig, says that he got his way in the teeth of some initial opposition from India's first Prime Minister, Jawaharlal Nehru, who preferred a less formal approach.

> We had six hundred princely states, who lived with an enormous amount of pomp, but the ceremony was oftentimes lacking. One of the things we've always appreciated about the British was their wonderful faculty of putting on spectacle of an official type and maintaining the solemnity of ceremonial. My husband, having been brought up in the British tradition, appreciated the military aspect of ceremonial, and this was one of the things he was able to introduce into the presidential household.
> The rituals of entertainment have also been retained. A banquet in the Pesident's palace today will in many ways resemble what it may have been in Mountbatten's time. The menu will be different. There will be little lights behind certain chairs to show that someone is a vegetarian and should not be served meat. There won't be a band in the gallery. But the rest of it is there: the gold plate that was left behind is still on display; the table napery and the decorations are very much as they were at that time.

1 The original Mughal capital, built by the Emperor Humayun in 1533.
2 The huge mosque opposite Delhi's Red Fort, built by the Emperor Shah Jahan in 1644.
3 One of the finest buildings of the Mughal period and the precursor of the Taj Mahal.

I can remember that Jawaharlal Nehru was very reluctant to conform to this ceremonial. Normally, for a state occasion, about a hundred guests would be invited; and he just wanted to come in with the chief guest and meet everybody casually, in the manner in which he did in his own home. But my husband insisted that everybody be lined up around the room and introduced, so that each person could meet the guest of honour and, at the same time, have a nod from the Prime Minister or the President. It was with great reluctance that he persuaded Nehru to accept this. Nehru practically threw a tantrum one day and said: 'I'm not going to have all this nonsense!' But once he did it, he recognised that it was a good thing, because all the guests met the guest of honour at least once and shook hands, and there would be a word or two said. That custom has been retained; and now, when a Chief of Protocol is faced with it, if he doesn't have a very good memory, he probably curses my husband.

While Tara Ali Baig welcomes the survival of viceregal ritual, she concedes that it has been an infliction on presidential spouses from a more rural and traditional background. But rural India, she says, has found ways of making its presence felt, even in such alien surroundings.

Our very first president came from Bihar, and his wife was a very orthodox, Hindu woman from a very rural background. She would have been much more at home in a hut than in this enormous palace in which she suddenly found herself. When she examined the kitchens, which were quite vast, she wanted them cleaned with cow-dung. This caused great woe and lamentation with the Military Secretary, who came to my husband in despair and said: 'For goodness sake, do something!' His next problem was that the two wings of the palace – the President's residence, on one side, and the guest-wing, on the other – enclose this magnificent garden; and she had all her pickles sunning happily on the verandah; so they had to find another, less visible place for her pickles.

Although the President has replaced the Viceroy as the Supreme Commander of the Indian Army, its officers are still the proudest guardians of imperial tradition. The regimental mess remains a bastion of British ritual, some of which, says General Palit, is a necessary morale-booster.

The armed forces have to have a certain discipline and cohesion. After all, it's only once or twice in many years that we fight, and yet we have to be ready to give our lives and to be trained for war. What the British might call bullshit is necessary in the army – polished buttons, crease down the middle of the trousers. Mess discipline is really aimed towards making fifteen or twenty brother officers, aged between fifty and eighteen, fight together; so there has to be a certain amount of ritual. It is a peculiarly British system, but it is translatable into Indian customs, too. We haven't done this;

we've just kept the old British traditions. In the matter of dress, we might have Indianised ourselves a little more. In the matter of eating habits, why we, who pride ourselves on eating with our fingers, the cleanest way of eating, have to stick to knives and forks – particularly today, made of stainless steel – I don't know. But otherwise, certain traditions that were particularly British – such as dining together once a fortnight at least, men only, not letting domestic influences invade the atmosphere of the mess – are, I think, very necessary.

Nevertheless, according to another retired general, Jagjit Singh Aurora, the days when army life revolved around polo and pig-sticking have had to give way to changes in military technology and to the fall in officers' salaries.

The training has altered, to deal with the newer weapons and techniques. Modern technology has made it imperative for both the men and the officers to learn many more things, and therefore one has to work much harder to master the profession, and you have to have an individual who's more intellectually inclined and need not be as fond of sports and social activities. There's less socialising and more serious soldiering. Also, because the cost of living has gone up and the pay hasn't really kept pace with it, an officer lives far more modestly than he did before. That does change your social outlook. The messes don't have the same number of social functions where people wear their dress uniform and that sort of thing. The food will be more frugal, and I don't think you will have the same number of servants running around.

An important colonial legacy has been the domination of the army by the so-called martial races of the north. Despite the setting up of some new, mixed units of guards and paratroopers, the old system of tribal regiments remains basically unchanged. 'We have our die-hards, too,' General Palit concedes. 'We loved our regiments, and we didn't want them broken up. The average army officer is conservative, and the reaction was: "Don't touch my regiment." So instead of being pro-integration, we were the worst of the lot. We kept our Sikhs, Mahrattas, Dogras, Gurkhas and what have you, all separate.'

The British introduced this regimental separation on the principle of divide and rule; and as Palit points out, the failure to develop a more integrated, national army after independence has had its advantages in keeping the military out of politics.

We are more apolitical than the British. The British armed forces have not always been apolitical: they killed their king. But compared with other armies, they have been apolitical, and they brought that system to us. The Indian Army has been almost by culture apolitical. Our caste system makes us apolitical, because the warrior caste may not govern, though it can reign. The prince is a warrior, and he serves in the army; but he may not take part in politics. So the Indian warrior caste was never politicised; and the British influence, combined with that tradition, has made us totally apolitical.

In independent India, as in the days of the Raj, the real guardians of power are not generals but civilians – the ministers and civil servants who occupy the two enormous Secretariat buildings, known as North and South Block, on either side of the presidential palace. And here, too, in a remarkable feat of colonial survival, the same ICS officers who had served the Raj hung on to the top jobs for almost three decades after independence. As a former Indian Foreign Secretary, Rajeshwar Dayal, remarks, the departure of the British half of the service left their Indian colleagues career opportunities far greater than they had known under the Raj.

Before independence, there were some Indians who rose to the top, who became members of the Viceroy's Executive Council, who retired with a knighthood. And if one was reasonably successful in one's career, one hoped that perhaps, one day, one might also retire with a knighthood. But it's obvious that, after independence, one's career prospects greatly expanded. When the Foreign Service was created in 1947, I and two of my brothers happened to be invited to join it by the Prime Minister. So this much wider horizon opened out before one, which one hadn't dreamt of before.

Despite such opportunities, some ICS officers found it difficult to adjust to political interference from the new Congress Raj. A. D. Gorwalla, the oldest surviving member of the ICS, tells the story of how his job as Supply Commissioner, responsible for controlling the prices of essential goods, brought him into conflict with an imperious Congress Chief Minister in Bombay.

We had controlled the price of sugar, but the price of *gur* or molasses rose; and so we controlled the price of *gur* also, to bring about parity between the two. The Chief Minister didn't like that at all; and he ordered, without even seeing the papers, that *gur* should be de-controlled. When the order came down to me, I re-submitted the whole case, saying: 'It seems that the facts of the case have not come to your notice.'
   The Chief Minister was very annoyed, and he sent for me and berated me. He said: 'You are my subordinate, and you dare to send back something on which I have passed orders?' I said: 'Sir, you didn't really know the facts when you passed the orders – you hadn't seen the papers – so I was duty-bound to re-submit the case to you. If you now decide, after considering all this, that you still want to de-control, of course your orders will be carried out. But it is my duty to give you the best advice on the subject possible.' He said: 'You are my servant. You have no business to say this, that or the other to me, only to carry out my orders.' I replied: 'Look, sir, there is a fallacy here. I am not your servant, nor is anyone else in

government any particular person's servant; he is a public servant. You are an elected public servant; I am an appointed public servant; but we are both servants. And the whole position of the Permanent Secretary is to be your expert adviser.' 'So you think I will now accept your views?' he asked. 'Yes, sir,' I said, 'I should think so.' 'Well,' he said, 'just to spite you, I won't, so you can see that my orders must be carried out.' I said: 'Please yourself, sir'; and I muttered to myself as I left the Gujerati saying: 'What can good sense do before power?'

Soon after this incident, Gorwalla resigned from the service rather than accept ministerial decisions which he considered biased in favour of private business interests. The vast majority of ICS officers, however, were more resilient and less scrupulous; and they succeeded in making themselves indispensable to the very politicians who had once threatened to abolish their service. Ashok Jaitley, a member of the Indian Administrative Service or IAS, formed after independence, accuses them of a certain lack of principle.

Here they were, earlier suppressing the same politician; and as he came into power, they not only adapted and adjusted, but were able to get round the politician, because they knew the system intimately. Here was this new boy, with all his ideas about what the country should be, and they were slowly able to dampen that fervour which was there on the day of independence and bring it down to the routine, mundane, operational level of administering a country. Jawaharlal Nehru had very categorically stated before independence that no change would be possible in this country unless the ICS mentality, the ICS Raj, was abolished. And yet, in the very first year after independence, the new government created the Indian Administrative Service in the image of the Indian Civil Service; and the ICS continued to occupy very senior positions and became the right-hand advisers to every senior politician. There was no induction from the political cadres into administration, as there has been in many other revolutionary situations.

Jaitley himself started his IAS career with a sense of awe about the ICS. But he claims that, after getting to know them better, he discovered many of them to be corrupt and inefficient with 'feet of clay'. Retired ICS survivors can be equally scathing about their IAS successors. They pride themselves on a long tradition of answering only to their own seniors; and this, claims Dharam Vir, a veteran administrator who retired as a provincial governor, made them better equipped to stand up to elected politicians than the new IAS cadre.

The ICS were supposed to be rulers of the country, and they were masters and functioned independently in their own way. The IAS came as civil servants, to work as servants of the people under political masters. And that did make for a lot of difference in approach and attitudes. It was very difficult for people of my service, even after independence, to take orders without questioning, if we didn't like them; and we did, all the time. The youngsters who came later were ground in the dust from the very beginning. They had to take orders and were not expected to argue too much. Some did, and they sometimes got into trouble for that; but most don't.

K. F. Rustamji, who has served as a senior police officer under both flags, makes a similar complaint about how political pressures affected his own service.

There was a greater inclination on the part of the British police officer to inspect, to tour, to attend to the minutiae of administration. He had more time for it, too. He didn't have to wait in the verandahs of ministers or spend hours in meetings. He was more on his own; and being the man on the spot, he was probably trusted more. The senior officer was never afraid of an instant transfer. He had the capacity to differ if he felt that he was in the right. He had a certain independence which he does not have today.

Whether in the civil service or the police, a major factor which undermined the superior attitudes and life styles of the past was the decline in officers' salaries after independence. While ICS salaries and pensions were guaranteed for life by covenant and stayed the same, the new IAS started off on considerably lower pay-scales. The privileged status of the old guard inevitably gave rise to some resentment, according to Dharam Vir.

As the number of IAS officers grew and the number of ICS officers dwindled, certain resentments, though not quite open, did arise. The IAS officers felt that they should be on the same level as the old ICS. But that couldn't be, because we belonged to a different era, which was expected to pass away after some time.

But one advantage of lower pay, says Ashok Jaitley, was that it left little room for the arrogance of the 'Heavenborn'.

A Secretary to the Government of India today, which is the highest post you can get to, still draws less than his equivalent in 1905. And if you consider the value of money then and the value of money today, that's a major gap. So there's been a tremendous change in lifestyles and attitudes between the IAS and the ICS. You see things much more from the worm's eye view, rather than the bird's eye view.

Although the IAS was set up in the same mould as the ICS, forty years of independence, says Jaitley, have brought some changes in the training and background of recruits.

The ICS went straight into the field after their one-year spell at Oxford or Cambridge. We now have an Academy of Administration, where you have a two-year training period and the subjects that you deal with are very different. There's much more economics and development, much more management. Now they're introducing computer sciences and systems analysis.

Among the ICS and the earlier batches of the IAS, the bulk of the recruits were from the urban middle-class. Over the years, there's been a change. For one thing, there is a reservation of 25 per cent of the annual intake for the Scheduled Castes and Tribes.[1] Secondly, there's been a larger number of people from rural areas coming into the service, with education spreading and the whole idea of a broader base to recruitment. Something in the region of 40 to 45 per cent today are from a rural background, which provides for a different kind of attitude to the problems of the villages.

Nevertheless, Ashok Jaitley, who is far from uncritical of his own cadre, argues that such changes have not been radical enough to create the kind of administration that an independent and avowedly socialist India requires.

It's true that the administrative structure built up and left to us by the British was responsible for a certain degree of continuity and stability and national integration, holding the country together. In fact, the ICS, after independence, were the ones who actually did the integrating of the princely states and so on, which had to be incorporated into the Union. But that continuity is now counter-productive to many things, including development. There is a growing body of opinion that the administration is just not good enough in dealing with problems like poverty. You cannot reach the last man, the really poor, because the distance is much too big, physically and otherwise. There is a great need today for a major overhaul in the administrative structure; and the old structure has outlived its utility.

Administrative reform has been a major theme of Indian politicians before and after independence, even though so little has actually been achieved. Both ICS and IAS officers, however, would agree that India's administrative problems owe less to bureaucratic inertia than to the drastic decline in the intellectual capacity and moral commitment of the political class that has governed since independence.

Elected politicians certainly ranked lowest in Lutyens's architectural scale, with their circular assembly building at the foot of the viceregal hill. Now the home of India's bicameral parliament, it was built for the far more exclusive Legislative Assembly of the Raj. And although that colonial legislature was elected on a restricted franchise, and had no formal control over the Viceroy's Cabinet, M. R. Masani, a veteran of many Indian parliaments, regards it as the best in which he ever served.

I was a member from 1945 to 1947. The Viceroy's Cabinet was not responsible to us. Even if we passed a vote of censure, they were

1 Under-privileged lower-caste and tribal groups who are listed for special provision in a schedule of the Constitution.

irremovable. That was the legal position; but I found that the behaviour of the Viceroy's councillors – who were mostly British and some Indian – was quite responsive, though not responsible. The debates were genuine; there was give and take.

I remember two occasions when my own speeches, which were quite offensive from the British point of view, evoked a very interesting response. One was when I demanded the release of Jayaprakash Narayan,[1] who was then in solitary confinement in Agra. Sir John Thorne, who was a crusty, old bureaucrat of the old type and the Home Member of the [Viceroy's] Council, came across to me and said: 'Let's talk about your friend. Would you like to see him?' I said: 'I'd love to, and he would also, because he's in solitary confinement.' He said: 'Well, go and spend a day with him.' 'Oh no,' I said, 'There's some trick in this. You want to spy on me and listen to our conversation.' He said: 'No, no. I will make sure that nobody is within sight or hearing when you're with your friend. But come back and tell me over lunch his state of mind.' When I came back, Sir John entertained me to lunch, and I gave him a picture of Jayaprakash's mind. 'He wouldn't do anything violent, would he?' he asked. I said: 'Of course not.' 'Oh, good,' he said. Jayaprakash was released within a few weeks of this conversation; and there's no doubt that it expedited his release. Now that is not the kind of thing that one expects today.

Similarly, when I supported the mutiny in the Royal Indian Navy in 1946, Philip Mason, who's still a friend of mine, was Defence Secretary. He, of course, replied to my speech, deprecating what I had said. But then, after the debate finished, he came over and shook hands and said: 'Let's sit down and talk. That was a wicked speech, Mr Masani, but I enjoyed every word of it!' This kind of very human response has been the basis of our friendship, which goes on to this day. So I would say that the Viceroy's councillors, though irremovable, were much more responsive to Opposition criticism than the present, so-called responsible ministers since independence.

The assemblies of the Raj, despite their limited powers, followed most of the conventions of Westminster; and as Masani describes, these were later adopted by the parliament of independent India.

The municipal corporations and the provincial assemblies were training grounds for people to mature for the Union Parliament. The Central Legislative Assembly was far more than a training ground; it was a darn sight *more* mature and evolved than the later *Lok Sabha*.[2] For instance, the role of the Speaker was very well established by the time power was transferred. We had a very good Speaker from 1945 to '47; and when the Interim Government came, Mr Nehru respected him and bowed to his decisions. So, by

1 A prominent leader of the Quit India movement.
2 The directly-elected lower house of the Indian Parliament.

the time the British retired, the institution of Speaker, which we took from them, was well established.

Although the office of Speaker survives intact, the over-zealousness of some of its occupants, according to Masani, can have amusing consequences.

Our so-called Speakers talked a hell of a lot; and a British member of parliament who visited the *Lok Sabha* said: 'Now I understand why he is called the Speaker, because he talks so much.' In 1967, I was Leader of the Opposition; and following British tradition, the then Prime Minister, Mrs Gandhi,[1] and I had to go to the seat of the member who had just been elected Speaker and drag him unwillingly to his seat as Speaker. But to my horror, the potential Speaker walked cheerfully to his seat, and the show was rather spoiled by his obvious readiness to take his seat without any reluctance whatsoever.

'We were very proud to be following the Westminster model in the early days,' says Masani and points to the excellent work done by parliamentary committees, formed on British lines to draft legislation and oversee public expenditure. Through the 1950s and '60s, M. R. Masani was regarded as one of Nehru's harshest parliamentary critics; but even he acknowledges that the credit for the survival of parliament must go to India's first Prime Minister.

He was much more in his seat in Parliament than Mrs Gandhi was later; and in that way, he showed more regard for Parliament than she did. Also, although we had a very splintered opposition, his response to opposition criticism, though quite often angry, was in the parliamentary tradition. I crossed swords with him on many occasions for about twelve years; and he took my speech seriously. He answered it, he rebutted what I said, he showed a little anger occasionally; but the fact that he did reply to the criticism and answer it, more or less point by point, showed that he cared for parliamentary criticism. So, by and large, he was a good Leader of the House.

I was in Parliament till 1970; and I found that, with every five years and a new election, the standard of debate deteriorated, the standard of education deteriorated, and quite frankly the standard of morality also deteriorated, because more and more corruption entered the ranks of members of parliament, who started selling licences and permits under the so-called socialist pattern. There's a lot of shouting and hooliganism, defying the Speaker when your time is up. When the Speaker asks you to sit down, you refuse to sit down. When he asks you to leave the House, you refuse to leave and the marshals have to be called in to lift you bodily. That kind of crude vulgarity has become part of our parliamentary life in the last

1 Nehru's daughter and political heir, Indira Gandhi, was Prime Minister from 1966 to 1977, and again from 1980 until her assassination in 1984.

few years. It started with Mrs Gandhi's prime ministership and
has got worse ever since. When I did not get re-elected in 1970,
some of those elected said I was very lucky, because I'd have been
disgusted with the new parliament, as compared with the earlier
one, where decorum was preserved and one got a good hearing.

Romesh Thapar, a left-wing political analyst, also dates the decline in
parliament to Mrs Gandhi's prime ministership. But he argues that such
problems are inherent in a society which remains deeply feudal in spirit,
with vast economic disparities.

I don't think you can plant a Westminster or American model on
India; you've really got to develop an Indian model, and this may
well dictate the need for a kind of consensus polity. The present
parliamentary system lives on vote-banks, based on tribe, caste and
community, unless there's some huge crisis like the Emergency.[1]
Then everybody sinks their differences and throws Mrs Gandhi
out; and then, when they want to bring her back, they do likewise.
The massive mandate is a kind of yearning for a credible system;
and the system has broken down today. It remains democratic, but
it's quite unlike a British or American democracy.
   The MPs themselves are men who have more or less criminal-
ised backgrounds. They're not respected for what they've done for
the country, but feared for what they can do in their constituen-
cies – whether they have enough suction in government to get
something done, and their links with the corrupted police. So it's a
very sleazy sort of parliamentary system. In fact, we're all the time
fighting for a quorum in parliament. They're all sitting around in
Delhi, but when a major issue comes up, only 40 or 50 MPs are
there. This is unforgivable, and it is largely due to the fact that
Mrs Gandhi used to avoid sitting through the sessions, although
her father was always present. Rajiv Gandhi[2] suffers from the
same problem. He does come more frequently than his mother,
but he's slightly aloof; he's not really part of the parliamentary
culture.

Thapar also points out that the British theory of cabinet government,
with collective responsibility to parliament, has become little more than
a constitutional fiction in the Indian context. And he blames Mrs
Gandhi, again, for concentrating all power and decision-making in the
Prime Minister's office. The result is an executive that has more in
common with the White House than with Whitehall. When Mrs Gandhi
became Prime Minister, she at least observed the constitutional conven-
tion of first being elected leader of the majority party in Parliament. But
when she was assassinated, even this formality was thrown to the

1 During the state of emergency (1975–77), Mrs Gandhi suspended civil liberties and
arrested her opponents. But she suffered a landslide defeat in the general election that
followed. Three years later, she was voted back into power by an equally large margin.
2 The third generation of a prime ministerial dynasty, Rajiv Gandhi, India's present
Prime Minister, succeeded his mother in 1984.

winds, and her son Rajiv was appointed to succeed her, although he had no official status in the party or the government.

Rajiv Gandhi, who was born in 1943, grew up without any memories of the Raj or of nationalist resistance to it. Like his grandfather, he went to Cambridge – though he returned without a degree – and several of his closest advisers are also Oxbridge products. But although they share the Western educational background of the generation that led India to independence, their knowledge of Indian conditions is far more limited. Arun Shourie, a prominent journalist of the younger generation, points out the limitations of his contemporaries in government.

> They are, of course, completely westernised. But what causes difficulties is not the fact that they have a Western upbringing or education, but the fact that they are completely unprepared for public issues, whether Eastern or Western. If you asked Rajiv Gandhi about Muslim personal law, which could become an issue involving violence in the next few years, he doesn't know whether the provision under discussion is from the Criminal Procedure Code enacted by the British in 1872, or from a judgement of the Supreme Court in 1985. He doesn't know, and all his Oxbridge friends don't know. It's not merely the fact that they are Western-educated that disables them, but that they have come in by helicopter and are suddenly in positions of responsibility. Contrast that with the type of people who assumed power when the British left. Pandit Nehru had been in prison for about nine years, and probably for seven years in solitary confinement, when he was doing nothing but reading and thinking about public issues.

Shourie sees the colonial political legacy as a mixed bag of British liberalism and British despotism. After all, civil liberties and representative institutions were not a gift from the colonial rulers, but had to be fought for by Indian nationalists. According to Shourie, later generations of Indian politicians have often preferred to emulate the more authoritarian practices of the Raj.

> Pandit Nehru tried to emulate the British practice at home, while a politician like Mrs Gandhi tried to emulate the British practice in the colonies. When I have to argue against an oppressive act of government, my instinct is to say: 'When Gandhiji was fighting British rule, he said such and such against the Rowlatt Acts,[1] and those Acts were very mild in comparison with what is being enacted now. So we must go by the values of the freedom struggle.' There was a difference in the practice of the British at home and of the colonial power in India; and the people who were fighting for India's freedom were always invoking the practices of the British at home.

[1] Enacted in 1919, the Rowlatt Acts gave the authorities wide emergency powers, and their repeal became a major nationalist demand.

The Constituent Assembly, which framed the republican, written constitution India adopted in 1950, was certainly more influenced by the existing colonial constitution, enacted by the Raj in 1935, than by the more liberal constitutional practice of Britain itself. One of its few surviving members, M. R. Masani, blames his Congress colleagues for deliberately retaining the strong centralist bias of viceregal rule, instead of introducing a genuinely federal structure, and for adopting the British electoral system, instead of proportional representation. Both decisions, he says, were designed to perpetuate over-centralised, one-party rule, at the expense of a more pluralistic system, better suited to Indian conditions.

We accepted the unitary system, because when the British were leaving India there was a unitary government of the Governor-General-in-Council. The governors of the provinces were really subordinate, rather like the French *préfect*. So we were not able to create a real federation because of the bias of the British to unitary government, what we had called contemptuously *Ma-Baap Sarkar*.[1] That tradition of paternalistic government was accepted by Nehru under the cloak of socialism.

The electoral system is one of the worst things we took from Britain, the first-past-the-post system. I was against it, and I argued for proportional representation. But the Congress leaders were rather short-sighted. They wanted power, and they felt that the first-past-the-post system would give them a majority out of proportion to their preponderance at the polls. When I argued that we might have governments which did not have a majority of the votes, one of them said: 'What does it matter? That's not very important. We don't want coalitions.' The mistake they made was to think that the British system would ensure a two-party system, which it hasn't. My argument was that we were Latins by temperament, not Anglo-Saxons – that we were a fissiparous people who would have eight or ten parties, whatever the system, which is what has happened. The result has been that, since independence to this day, never has a government in Delhi enjoyed a 50 per cent vote of the public. They've been governments with 40 per cent or so of the vote, but with two-thirds of the seats in Parliament, enabling them to amend the Constitution. This has been a disaster, particularly when there are linguistic and religious minorities which need protection.

At the other end of the political spectrum, the Marxist Chief Minister of West Bengal, Jyoti Basu, also criticises India's new Congress rulers for taking over some of the more negative features of the Raj, not least its repressive law-and-order apparatus.

We are not wholly for the Constitution, which we call a bourgeois constitution. What they had condemned earlier, during the freedom

1 Mother-Father government.

struggle, they later adopted from the British. Nehru used to be very forthright in the early years, during the fight for independence. But when he came into government, from the first day they were adapting all those British criminal laws to detain people without trial; and in two or three parts of India, including Bengal, our party was declared illegal soon after independence in 1947.

The ills of India's parliamentary democracy cannot be separated from the kind of economic development that has taken place during and since the Raj. Most critics, whether on the left or the right, agree that it is the nexus between corrupt politicians and corrupt businessmen that often makes such a travesty of democratic procedures. Large-scale political and economic corruption first reared its head in the last years of the Raj, during the Second World War, when India's new business class was able to rake in huge untaxed profits; and corruption remained the price of the rapid industrial growth that took place after independence.

The 'Permit-Licence Raj', as Nehru's system of state-controlled economic planning was called, has been blamed for many of the ills of India's political and economic life. But the technological revolution India has achieved, with active state participation, would have been inconceivable in the days of colonial *laissez-faire*, when policy-makers did their best to keep government out of the economy. As Prakash Tandon, a veteran manager of private industry, reminds us, even the colonial regime, during its final years, had recognised the inevitability of an expanding public sector; and Nehru's ambitious Five-Year Plans were able to build on a British blueprint.

The manufacturing public sector began in the late nineteenth century, with the setting up of a number of railway workshops; so the railways were the pioneers. Then, during the war in 1945, it's a very little known fact that the British government in India came out with a White Paper on post-war industrial policy. It advocated that post-war industrial development would have to be balanced in different sectors and that heavy industry would be as important as light industries. But since heavy industry may not draw private capital, because gestation is long and the profits low, government would have to step in. That was the genesis of the Indian public sector; and, in fact, they drew up a list of industries like defence, shipping and steel which would be public sector. The White Paper divided industry into three parts; those in which the state alone would operate, those which would be mixed, and those that would be left exclusively to the private sector. This was to be the entire basis of Nehru's policy.

Despite the socialist rhetoric of Congress, Nehru's public sector has best served the interests of the country's business class, with its control of the political purse-strings. The alliance between Congress and Indian business dates back to Gandhi's *Swadeshi* movement; and independence allowed the business houses who had invested in nationalism to cash in

on rapid growth. As Indian industrialists started manufacturing everything from cars to nuclear energy, British firms, suddenly deprived of
their favoured status under the Raj, sometimes found it hard to adapt, as
Prakash Tandon, who worked for Lever Brothers, recalls.

> The story goes that, after independence, a managing agency
> chairman of Calcutta wrote a long letter to his home office relating
> his woes under the new government. Back came a very terse cable:
> 'Appreciate your problems. Suggest you meet the Viceroy.' He
> hadn't got used to the fact that there was no Viceroy any longer,
> and the cable was a hint to go and talk to the authorities that were
> and not miss those that had gone. I remember, even in our own
> firm, we had to make certain changes – send some of the old types
> back and bring in some younger people who had no feelings one
> way or the other.

Though most British firms were quick to make their peace with the
new rulers, many nonetheless found themselves edged out or taken over,
often by Indian industrialists who had started as their commercial agents.
While Indian businessmen welcomed foreign collaboration after independence, their new partners tended to be Japanese, German and
American multinationals, who were usually more generous about sharing
their know-how than the older British companies.

The fruits of such economic development have gone predictably to the
middle classes who led the nationalist movement, not to the masses in
whose name they fought. Yet critics of the present system, like the left-
wing economist Ashok Mitra, acknowledge that India as a whole is today
economically far better off than under colonial rule.

> We have fairly reliable statistics from the beginning of the twentieth
> century, and they show that, between 1900 and the time of
> independence, *per capita* income was stagnant. Whatever improve-
> ment in the levels of living have taken place have been since the
> early 1950s. It could be that, in patches here and there, land
> problems have intensified; but overall, there is no question that
> things were very much worse during the British days.

Along with pockets of nostalgia among the narrow élites who
prospered under it, the Raj left behind wide extremes of poverty and
wealth and serious divisions between town and countryside. The colonial
rulers had neither the will nor the resources to modernise India's
antiquated, feudal agriculture or to bring educational and health facilities
to the villages. Instead they invested in the urban middle classes, through
whom progress was expected to filter down to the deprived masses. The
growing gap between India's rich and poor and the unresponsiveness of
parliamentary institutions may have belied such expectations; but the
Raj did leave behind at least two middle-class institutions which could,
despite their shortcomings, be turned to the defence of the underdog –
the courts and the press.

The Indian judicial system remains almost identical to that bequeathed by the British; and its complexity and conservatism has many critics. S. K. Acharyya, Advocate-General of West Bengal, condemned it as a lawyers' paradise shortly before his death in 1986.

It has outlived its purpose. The sooner these courts vanish and you have a People's Court, where a common man can come and judge the case of another common man, the better. The whole thing is a paradise for the lawyers to mint money. When the Constitution was being framed, I was flabbergasted to see so many Articles in it. I asked N. C. Chatterji, who was an MP and also a good lawyer, why the Constitution dealt with sales tax and the Public Service Commission and details like that. He said: 'Don't be a fool, my son. For every word that is written there in the Constitution, all of us will make more than 500 gold mohurs[1] a day.' The constitution and the laws in it are a boon given to the vultures wearing the black coat and gown, so they can pick on the flesh of the common man.

Justice is the first casualty, because if you are just and truthful, you will never win your case. You must intelligently mix truth with lies and manufacture evidence; otherwise you have no chance. A village dispute should really be decided by a tribunal appointed by the villagers themselves. They will know the litigants so intimately that they can come to the truth. But here, in the air-conditioned rooms of Calcutta High Court, they cannot do that.

The judiciary itself has come under fire in recent years for a decline in integrity and independence. H. M. Seervai, a former Advocate-General of Bombay, reflects on the falling standards.

By a queer quirk of history, the salary of judges was fixed in a schedule to the Constitution. Judges were paid 3500 rupees in the High Court in 1950, and they were paid the same amount in 1982; so it has become practically impossible to get first-class men to go on the Bench. Low salaries in the subordinate courts were always a source of corruption, especially in the criminal courts after smuggling and trafficking in drugs came along on an extensive scale. Corruption had not, broadly speaking, reached the High Courts; but I am afraid it has crept in and, unless steps are taken to eliminate it, it is likely to increase.

Another British-trained, retired Advocate-General, Govind Swaminathan of Madras, suggests that the Indianisation of the Bench has inevitably meant some decline in impartiality.

Judges today are not as independent. They're sons of the soil dealing with sons of the soil; whereas, before independence, they were Britishers dealing with what to them was always a foreign country. Now, unfortunately, they sometimes carry with them the natural prejudices that they have in private life on to the Bench. For

1 A Mughal coin valued at fifteen British Indian rupees and used, like the British guinea, in calculating barristers' fees.

example, you know a judge is anti-birth-control; or you know a judge is a very religious chap who visits temples; or you know a judge is a Christian; so you're careful how you argue before them.

According to Swaminathan, the survival of English as the language of the higher courts has also created unnecessary problems for litigants and the legal profession itself.

The young man of today, who has joined the Bar within the last five years, may be very clever and able but just cannot express himself adequately in the English language; whereas people of 20 to 25 years' standing can't possibly argue a case in Tamil, the language of this state. In the lower courts, judgements are all in Tamil, evidence is all in Tamil. And whenever clients come to me with that kind of thing, I have to say: 'I'm sorry, but unless you get it translated for me, I can't do a thing for you.' Fortunately, I've got a bunch of wonderful juniors who shield me all the time from this kind of embarrassment.

A major limitation on judicial independence has been the right of central Government to nominate senior judges. S. K. Acharyya voiced a widespread concern that this has been increasingly abused for political ends.

Nowadays it is the habit of the Union Government to pack the benches, whether in the state High Courts or the Supreme Court, with the judges of their choice. So, in the great fight that's going on over whether India is a federal or unitary system, you will find the judges always leaning over backwards to try and support the Union Government. Before independence, a person who had a good practice and was known at the Bar as an up-and-coming lawyer would have a chance of being elevated to the Bench. But now anybody can be elevated to the Bench, provided he toes the line of the central Government.

Despite such political constraints, the old High Courts established by the Raj have demonstrated a capacity to check abuses of executive power. H. M. Seervai tells the story of how the Bombay High Court championed the rights of slum-dwellers against arbitrary eviction by the state.

For years and years, a large number of people lived on the roads and pavements, slept in huge pipes meant to transport water; and children were brought up on the pavements. All of a sudden, it occurred to a Chief Minister, in the height of the monsoon, to direct quite illegally that they should be transported out of Bombay. When this came to be known, counsel rushed up to the High Court, and the High Court granted a stay. The matter was carried by the municipality and the government to the Supreme Court. After a full argument, the Supreme Court went to the farthest limit to which it could rationally go. About four or five years had passed; and the

Supreme Court held that, before any person is removed, he must be
given an opportunity of being heard; and they made a strong
recommendation to government to see that some alternative
accommodation was provided. Now people may look upon this as
a waste of time; but it was not, because the government
subsequently came out with a scheme acknowledging its obligation
to provide accommodation to these people.

The finest hour of the High Courts was during the Emergency of
1975–77, when Prime Minister Indira Gandhi virtually suspended all
civil rights guaranteed by the Constitution. In a sense, it was the
Allahabad High Court which provoked the declaration of emergency
when it found Mrs Gandhi guilty of election malpractice and barred her
from office. During the next two years, there were several similar
instances of independent judges who refused to be cowed by executive
power and acted as a brake on government censorship and arbitrary
arrest.

The Emergency also showed certain sections of the Indian press
standing up to government pressure. Their independence probably owed
less to British ideals of editorial freedom than to the experience they had
gained under the Raj of resisting British censorship with British
arguments. According to Cusrow Irani of the once British-owned
Calcutta *Statesman*, press freedom in India remains, as it was during the
Raj, a question of journalistic choice.

> During the Emergency, Government first tried to take over control
> of our Board of Directors on an absurd interpretation of the
> Companies Act. We knocked that back, and they didn't succeed.
> Then they tried to attack editorial integrity directly by insisting
> what we should carry; and I said publicly that I did not understand
> a form of censorship that asks you to say something. That caused a
> furore. Then they applied financial pressures by withdrawing not
> only their own advertising but organising a boycott of private
> advertising. If the Emergency had lasted another six months, I don't
> think we would have been able to continue.
>
> Even now, Government continues to have a monopoly of
> newsprint supplies. Government still insists on sitting in judgement
> on advertising rates. Government itself is the biggest advertiser and
> manipulates this blatantly to their advantage. But I have to say that
> the Indian press today has no direct form of pressure, in terms of
> 'You will publish this' or 'You will not publish that.' It's a question
> of whether you are prepared to pay the price for your independ-
> ence. The Indian press is today as free as it chooses to be; but it
> doesn't always demonstrate its willingness to be free.

Romesh Thapar, who started his journalistic career under a British
editor, thinks that the Indian press today is less government-oriented
than it was in colonial times; but he feels that the product has
deteriorated in some other respects.

There is more in-depth coverage now than there was in those days. Then everything was an official hand-out or something you didn't really chase because it was embarrassing to the occupying power. But I think the detailed attention to the quality of the newspaper – the quality of writing and proofing – has deteriorated. There is a laziness in approach. The senior staff come to office at 9.30 or 10; they hold their little confabulation about the day's work; and by 5 o'clock they're closing up and pushing off, irrespective of what's happening, and very seldom coming back. Now, that's something we never used to do in the old days. If there was a big newsbreak, we were back in the office at 11 at night, and all of us were exchanging ideas, updating the editorials, thinking of the front-page display. This does *not* happen any more.

Mehra Masani, who helped set up All India Radio before independence, complains of a similar lack of imagination and initiative in the broadcasting media; and she blames the interference of ministers and bureaucrats in day-to-day programming.

The programme producer today does not feel free to put on air a play or piece of music which he considers good. He must take into account the prejudices and tastes of people up above. We had one minister who really ran broadcasting as if he were the Director-General. He would decide who would sing in the national programme of music and whether a play was good or bad. This naturally meant that the programme officer was always looking back over his shoulder to find out whether the great god in the ministry would approve. All kinds of programmes were put on the air for which there was no audience at all, because they just wanted to oblige somebody. If a literary programme started by the minister was unpopular, it didn't make any difference. It would go on being repeated, year after year, simply because he wanted it.

When people asked me which were the best days for broadcasting, I used to say: 'Till independence'; the reason being that Sir Andrew Clow[1] wouldn't allow Quit India to be broadcast or any kind of subversion of the Raj; but beyond that, he was not interested in whether we broadcast light music or classical music. He left this to the Indians who were running broadcasting. So there was interference on the political level in British days: the news bulletins could not report at length what Gandhi or Nehru said. But on the other hand, as far as the non-political broadcasts were concerned, we had no interference whatsoever. That was *not* the case after independence.

One of the major criticisms I level against the present system is that one would imagine nothing had changed. We got a whole lot of Indian bosses in place of the Englishmen, but otherwise the programmes just carried on as they were – the programme pattern

1 Member for Communications and Broadcasting in the Viceroy's Cabinet.

remains to this day what it was in 1938. With independence, there should have been a great deal more political comment and dissenting opinions. But my idea of independence was obviously very different from that of the people who came to power. They just thought that they would take over this functioning medium and use it as a good propaganda tool.

The political incentives which led the Raj to keep Indian broadcasting under direct government control are, if anything, far more compelling today, when even poorer households in the villages have at least a transistor-radio. But state control of information in India remains far from monolithic, especially if one considers the massive expansion of privately-owned printed media, keeping pace with growing literacy. The last forty years have brought much official patronage for India's national language, Hindi, and also for the many regional vernaculars. And yet, as Cusrow Irani confirms, the English-language press has also prospered and grown, with a readership now that is far larger than in British times.

The demand for English-language papers is growing; and the opinion-making newspapers are almost exclusively, even today, in the English language. English is about the only language that Indians in different parts of the country can communicate with today. You may not be proud of it, but it is a reality. There are fourteen major languages recognised in the Constitution and hundreds of dialects; and there is a great deal of jealousy as far as Hindi is concerned in the non-Hindi-speaking areas. People in the south have died for their language; but English is more readily accepted on the basis of a doctrine of equal disability.

Whether one regards it as an asset or a disability, the English language remains the most enduring and pervasive legacy of the old Raj to the new. Politically, it represents a necessary compromise between India's linguistically diverse sub-nationalities, and its survival as the official 'link-language' is guaranteed by special legislation. It is the language of central government and the higher courts, of university education and the major professions. And yet, it poses as much of an educational and cultural dilemma now as it did for the nineteenth-century British reformers who introduced it.

ABIDE WITH ME
THE NEW ANGLO-INDIANS

You cannot be a major figure in India if you are not proficient in English. If you do not know English, you are unlikely to be anything more than a social worker, and you may be honoured as such, but you will never be able to rise into the professions and make your name nationally. This is what we call the English-speaking élite, asserting itself at every level.

Romesh Thapar (journalist and political analyst)

The Western education with which the Raj first set out to court the Indian middle classes remains the most important avenue of success in independent India, a passport to senior jobs and status, at home and abroad; and its medium of instruction, the English language, is still the precious *lingua franca* of the country's rulers. The last of the British headmasters have passed on; but at places like Bombay's Cathedral School, their Indian successors try and emulate the traditions they left behind. Cathedral's present principal, Colonel Eric Simeon, is an Indian Christian of the pre-independence generation. He points out that the syllabus today puts far more emphasis on Indian history and languages than it did in the 1930s, when he was at school. But Bombay's first high school is still the exclusive preserve of its most westernised and affluent citizens; and such continuity is emphasised by its Anglican ritual.

> We still have the old school uniform: the boys wear ties coloured house-wise, and the girls have skirts with girdles showing their house-colours. . . . A school like ours, allied to the Church, has got very strong traditions after 125 years. We have kept the old house names, because changing them would be a great disappointment and not very popular. At our assembly, we still have hymns, we still say the Lord's Prayer, and every child here accepts that. On certain days, like Ash Wednesday, we have a service in the Cathedral and sing well-known carols. Our Founder's Day service is always held in the Cathedral. The Bishop takes a very active role, and the whole choir is augmented by our girls and boys. We process in and out; it's quite a solemn thing, and very moving.

Founded and still managed by the Anglican Church, Cathedral is perhaps less typical of upper-class Indian education today than its younger northern rival, the Doon School. Established in 1935, with sponsorship from Indian princes and business magnates, the Doon is a boarding school which combines a more Indian cultural ethos with the public-school discipline introduced by former British headmasters. Colonel Simeon was a master there before he became Principal of Cathedral, and he comments on the differences and similarities.

The Doon School certainly is more Indian. They have an Indian orchestra, and the assembly songs are all sung in Hindi with Indian music. The food is entirely Indian, and the boys are encouraged to wear Indian clothes in the evening. They are allowed to speak their own language, and quite a lot of them speak Hindi among themselves; whereas I don't think you'll find a Cathedralite speaking in any language other than English.

Nevertheless, the prefectorial system and the house system at Doon were inherited from the British, the idea being to have healthy competition and to give chances for leadership. The system of housemasters and tutors is more effective there, because it is a boarding school. . . . The Doon School old-boy network also takes a lot of beating, even by schools in England. They have kept it alive with an up-to-date directory giving names and addresses and what old boys have done. And the Doon has produced leaders in almost every sphere of Indian life.

With Prime Minister Rajiv Gandhi and some of his closest advisers among its alumni, the Doon epitomises the power of an Indian public-school network, known less politely as the 'Dosco Mafia'. Despite the massive expansion of Indian higher education in the last forty years, older schools like Cathedral and Doon remain privileged stepping-stones to the more élite colleges. One obvious reason for their success is the facilities they can afford compared with the average state school. Kamla Bhasin, who now holds a senior United Nations job, says that her father, a small-town doctor in Rajasthan, could not possibly have afforded the fees of a private school; so she went to the local Hindi-medium state school. She lists the disadvantages she has had to overcome.

Some of the rooms were incomplete and part of the roof was missing, because they had run out of money. In some classrooms, there were two classes, so the physical arrangements for our seating were really bad. The number of teachers was always inadequate, and their training was not very good. Most of them were doing it, not because they liked teaching, but because this was the only job they could get.

I remember doing geography without ever having a globe in the room, or even proper maps, and doing science without a laboratory. There were no proper playgrounds, no craft facilities; and this would be the situation of most government schools in the rural areas.

We started English when we were about eleven, with the usual 'C-A-T, cat, B-A-T, bat, and R-A-T, rat'. It was a terrible way to learn, although some of the teachers were really very innovative. If the teacher wanted to teach us that in 'chalk' the 'l' is silent, he would make a story out of it. He would say: 'Listen, "l" is Lallu, the younger brother, and "k" is Kaka, the older brother. When the elder brother is there, the younger brother shuts up. So when it is "lk" in chalk, you say "chawk".' We never forgot that once we had learnt it. But it was really bad English. I remember that, when we were in Grade 9 and had done English for four years, a new teacher came and asked us to repeat the alphabet; and 90 per cent of the children couldn't repeat it up to 'z'.

English, according to Kamla Bhasin, has an importance far beyond language; and it is a yardstick of social status and success.

With the English-medium education goes a whole set of goodies. Saying that you are English-medium means that your parents earned enough to send you to a private school. At a private school in Rajasthan, the monthly cost would have been 500 rupees, which was the entire salary of my father. So English-medium assumes you belong to a certain class, and you have all the advantages of that class. You have the advantage of a network of old boys and girls which puts you in touch with the ruling élite, and that's why there is this great charm of the English language.

Like Kamla Bhasin, students from Indian-medium schools can and do reach university; but here, too, with English as the medium of instruction, they find themselves at a serious disadvantage. As Romesh Thapar points out, the problem is worse because so many of the teachers would themselves be far more at home in their Indian mother-tongues.

You are getting the growth of an Indian English, which is really not a language that is properly taught any more. It comes out as a mixture of pronunciation, and many words mean different things. . . . Very few of the people who are giving lectures in English really know how to speak the language now, and the students don't really know the meaning of so many words. So the whole communication between teacher and student breaks down, and they have to spend hours trying to study their textbooks by rote. If you saw an Indian college student's textbook, he would mark many English words and then write on the side in his mother-tongue what they mean. So you can imagine what is happening to the mind of India when it is being robbed of language.

The resulting intellectual loss is reflected in an alarming decline of university standards. An academic of the old school, Professor G. C. Bannerji of Bombay, describes a depressing visit to one of India's newer universities.

I went on a small inspection committee to the University of Gujerat, and the Vice-Chancellor showed me round the library. While he was talking to the librarian, I happened to see a shelf on which new books had been catalogued and placed. The pages of the books were still uncut, because they had not been used; but they had been bought because the money had been allocated. We are going through this sort of farce on a very big scale: books are bought and not used.

Like other Indians who have a stake in the promotion of good English, Bannerji believes that the colonial legacy has been a mixed blessing. While it has left the English language firmly entrenched as a medium of instruction, the teaching of English itself has been taken for granted and neglected. The number of Indians speaking English of a sort has expanded dramatically since the Raj, not least because of the access it provides to the international job market; but the numbers who know the language well remain small. Both English and education generally, argues Bannerji, would fare better if the regional mother-tongues became the medium of instruction and English was taught instead to those who really wanted it.

> The average standard of English is now so poor that it is no longer a standard. . . . Those who have been brought up to learn English in the vernacular-medium schools may write fairly well, but they cannot express themselves orally, they don't know the spoken language. . . . That is why we must learn how to teach English to adults, because the biggest weakness in the chain of communication between the teacher and student is that the teacher is less and less able to impart what could be called respectable English. . . . But the best way to learn a language is still with the mother's milk. In geographical areas where people speak the same vernacular language, it is much less difficult for them to make progress in the writing and publishing of books, and therefore in imparting education, in their mother-tongue. The northern heartland, for instance, is more or less Hindi-speaking. People there use the language well and would prefer to teach in Hindi, rather than English.

The post-independence period has seen the emergence of a new generation of Indian writers, labelled the 'Indo-Anglians', for whom English is a mother-tongue, if only by adoption. But a leading Indo-Anglian poet, Adil Jussawalla, argues that Indian English, unlike its American equivalent, does not qualify as a distinctive and creative language.

> What's different about it from British English is not standardised. It's not as though we make the same deviations from British English all over the country. It's just that we've been taught the language badly and make errors of grammar and syntax. So I don't think there's an Indian English. . . . My own preference is for the correct usage of English, rather than experiments in Indian English writing. Often a writer doesn't know the language well enough to be able to make that experiment and it becomes a way of saying: 'Why should anyone criticise the way I write?' By and large, those of us who write in English will have to use a norm which is as close to British English as it can be. . . . It's a tragedy that we haven't realised that we should regard English as a foreign language and teach it as such, using all the latest techniques, like language-labs and direct-method teaching, instead of just assuming that English comes naturally to us.

But English, according to Professor Bannerji, has become so important a status-symbol that its replacement as the medium of instruction is often seen as a threat by the very groups who might be expected to benefit most from a switch to the vernaculars.

> The Deputy Registrar of Bombay University told me that he visited a District Local Board, where the chairman said: 'I hear you have plans to switch over to Marathi[1] as the medium of instruction for our children. Do you now want to leave us out in the cold? Take care, because if you do that, you will know which side we're on.' This may be misconceived, but it is true. Jobs in Bombay are available to those who know English, and jobs are not available to those who don't know English or know it very badly. This is a cold fact.

Like Latin in medieval Europe, English means power in India today. The alternative would be a massive translation of higher education into India's many regional mother-tongues, an option ruled out by nineteenth-century British Indian educationists for reasons both financial and ideological. Romesh Thapar laments the persistence of such colonial attitudes today.

> The mother-tongues have been ignored, because we haven't done adequate translation of world literature into them. Nobody can survive on his mother-tongue if he can't get at the knowledge of the world. Translation should have been one of the major enterprises of free India; but it is nil, and nobody can live off translation today. Instead, Indian English is everybody's great desire, not only to be understood around the country, but also to move around the world. You go to Punjab, and they say: 'We have got many convents.' 'What?' you ask. 'The Catholic Church is all over the place?' 'No, no,' they say, 'the schools which teach English, we call them convents.' And if you ask: 'Why do you teach English?' they look surprised and say: 'Don't you know about international mobility?' So the millions of India are picking up the English language in order to penetrate the world.

The colonial hangover is reflected, too, in textbooks which are often hopelessly out of date or inappropriate. Professor Bannerji cites a particularly ludicrous example.

> A fairly senior officer in the Education Department went to see a girls' school which catered for the upper class. He looked at a geography textbook, and the first sentence said: 'Our country is an island.' When he asked the teacher, she was flustered and couldn't explain. He looked up the publisher's imprint, and it turned out to be a geography book meant for English children. This sort of mistake does occur.

Amid the confusion and mediocrity of Indian higher education today, there remain islands of academic excellence; and they, not surprisingly,

1 The regional language of the state of Maharashtra, of which Bombay is the capital.

tend to be the older, colonial institutions. As Bannerji points out, places like Bombay's Elphinstone College, of which he was principal, command a snob-value that goes beyond academic considerations.

Bombay University maintains its reputation, not for its intrinsic virtues, but the fact that it has been a university for so long and acquired a reputation by the mere efflux of time. A possible employer would like to have a chap from Elphinstone College, rather than a college which has been working for only the last two years. When I went to see the Principal of Poona Engineering College and told him I came from Elphinstone, he said: 'I'm sorry, I don't know Elphinstone College; but I know the Engineering College, and it's older than yours.' The Poona Engineering College was started in 1834, and it's the oldest teaching institution in engineering in the whole of the Bombay Presidency. A man who stood first in the degree there had a standing offer of an engineer's job with the Government of Bombay.

The old English saying 'Birds of a feather flock together' remains profoundly true. The Cathedral School, which is regarded as the best high school in Bombay, has boys of a certain social status and income-group, and their parents value the veneer of education and take the trouble to see that their children get into the older colleges like Elphinstone, St Xavier's or Wilson in Bombay, or St Stephen's College in Delhi.

Even more than the Bombay colleges, St Stephen's in Delhi has a reputation for living in its missionary past. Dileep Simeon, the son of Cathedral's principal and now a university lecturer, was a student there in the 1960s.

It was set up by the Cambridge Mission, and it's a Christian-run institution. The students, by and large, came from the professional and bureaucratic élite of northern India. It had a certain aura about it, of being the place where the children of powerful people went. If you acquired a degree there, you would automatically become a member of the ruling hierarchy in the country.

Even the architecture of its modern campus was supposed to be reminiscent of Oxbridge, and the whole idea of education there was modelled on Oxford and Cambridge. There were tutors; the hostels were referred to as halls of residence. When you came in to eat dinner, you would have to bow to the High Table, and the person sitting at the head of the High Table would nod in your direction. Grace would be said before eating. It was all very, very reminiscent of a hall in some English college.

My tutor was a gentleman called Pearson, whom I respected more out of fear than liking. He worked there for no salary at all, because he owned stocks and shares and tea-gardens. He was definitely a remnant of colonial times, and his attitude towards us was quite contemptuous. But he was a pillar of the college, in charge of literary activities, and a very important figure who set the tone.

One felt completely as if one was living in some kind of ivory tower. And this came out most blatantly when I was a member of a team which visited Bihar during the famine of 1967. That came as a kind of thunderclap in my consciousness, because I could never have imagined that those were the conditions prevailing in India.

Despite such criticisms, the colonial aura of India's older universities still has its guardians in the teaching faculties. Malcolm Adiseshiah describes the unexpected resistance he encountered when, as Vice-Chancellor of Madras University, he attempted to Indianise its convocation ceremony.

We wore the gown and the hood: and then the senators joined together, with the Chancellor present to say grace; and then we went marching into the convocation-hall to British music. When I became Vice-Chancellor, I couldn't stand it. I said: 'After all these years, this means nothing to the majority of students.' So I brought in Indian music and made a few changes. But there was resistance from the teachers, because they were used to the old British way of doing things and thought I was diluting standards. The whole infrastructure that we had of professors, readers and lecturers, the academic hierarchy, the boards of studies, the methodology of research, all this had just carried over from what happens in Oxford and Cambridge.

Colonial ritual might be a harmless and colourful evocation of past traditions if it were not so alien and oppressive to students from less privileged backgrounds. It legitimises new forms of discrimination which can be even more cruel than those of the old Anglo-Indians. Kamla Bhasin, for instance, remains bitter about the treatment that she and many others received from English-speaking fellow students. 'They took pride in not speaking their own language and made fun of you if you didn't speak English. In college, we girls who were not from the English-medium schools were called "Behenjis".'[1] Dileep Simeon, one of the privileged English-speaking minority, confirms that college life can be deeply divided by such tensions between language groups.

Willy-nilly, a kind of cleavage seems to develop between them. They don't communicate much, and the tension may erupt at particular moments when they do rub shoulders. The English-speaking students, even now, refer to the others as 'HMTs' or 'Hindi-medium types'; and there's a tone of contempt there.

The dominance of the English-speaking élite goes beyond mere social snobbery. As Professor Bannerji explains, it can involve a near monopoly of college life, inside and outside the classrooms, by the more anglicised.

In a college like Elphinstone you find that the places of importance

[1] Hindi for 'sister', but used in a derogatory and insulting sense.

– the dramatic society, the film society, the debating society – are all monopolised by the students from Anglo-Indian schools. I have had letters from other students after they left college saying: 'You should look more deeply at how we suffered, how we were excluded from all useful and enjoyable activities. We could not even form a group of our own, because we were not homogeneous.'

As in colonial times, the more affluent and successful Indian students tend to have their sights fixed on Western universities, except that the United States now exerts a stronger pull than Oxbridge. According to Arun Shourie, such aspirations are often encouraged by parents who missed out: 'My father, who worked for government, might have felt in his youth that, if only he had been able to go to England, he would have made it into the ICS; because people who were not as bright as him made it merely because they could go to England. That probably influenced his urge for his children.' The metropolitan attractions of the West, says Shourie, fostered a mindless contempt for things Indian among some of his student contemporaries: 'A number of my friends would carry *Encounter* or the London *Times* under their arms in the coffee- houses; and for them denigration and ignorance of our own tradition was the mark of culture.'

Such complaints about a colonial 'slave-mentality' are echoed by older champions of nationalist education like Rukmini Devi Arundale and Sankara Menon of the Madras Theosophical Society, who argue that resistance to Anglo-Indian values was far stronger in colonial times. Rukmini Devi was the last representative of India's colonial renaissance; and a few months before her death in 1986, she lamented the continuing stranglehold of an Anglo-Indian education which lacks either an aesthetic sense or any relevance to Indian conditions. 'In the past, there was opposition to the British due to the freedom movement; but now, there's no opposition. American films and television have taken over the lives of people, and the result is not only un-Indian but a mixture of everything.'

Rukmini Devi's deputy, Sankara Menon, explains the difference between westernisation then and now.

In those days, people spoke excellent English, much better English than most Indians talk today. But in their personal lives, they were still very Indian. When the British were here, Indians were more Indian than they have been after independence. The British did not seriously dislodge us from our own religions and philosophies; we were not seriously tampered with. Our anglicism was not quite so mordant or pressing as the type we get now.

Today the media are heavily anti-nationalistic, from the point of view of Indian culture. The cinema, for example, may give you Indian stories, but the whole technique, the way they think about their plots and sequences, is Western. The film music, too: they want to have harmony and counterpoint and don't know how to bring it in; so you get a horrible, forced marriage between East and West, and such things don't produce good offspring.

The high school and arts academy run by the Madras theosophists at Kalakshetra has tried to reconcile a modern syllabus with the intimacy and simplicity of the traditional *guru* system. Although it remains an élite oasis of aesthetic education for those who can afford it, Kalakshetra, like Tagore's Santiniketan, did represent a search for Indian alternatives to colonial education. In the post-independence period, such experimentation and innovation are rare.

According to a former nationalist firebrand, Aruna Asaf Ali, the difference between her generation and young Indians today is not really over the extent of westernisation, but the quality and depth of the Western values adopted.

> British education emancipated our leaders. We were brought into direct contact with modern, twentieth-century developments; and that was a tremendous thing. The English language itself helped us to read and think beyond our four corners. In fact, looking back, I tell many young people: 'The British did a great deal of good by teaching us what they did, because we took up the challenge, we became different people, we grew mentally, and we got the fundamentals of liberty, equality, fraternity, all those socialist values. We were anglicised; but you people, who were born after freedom, are anglicised only in the externals, and you have not grown. Although you speak English, you've taken only the superficial aspects of Western civilisation.'

It is a generation gap due partly to the fact that much Western influence in India today is American rather than British. And there are younger Indians, like Arun Shourie, who agree that the change has been for the worse. 'The urban middle-class culture today is a vulgarised form of what they take to be Western culture. It is certainly overwhelmingly Western in aspiration, in terms of wanting to acquire Western consumer goods. But it is a sort of Punjabi-Texan culture – a rapacious culture, in consumer patterns as well as in the use of concrete and the unplanned, Western-type architecture that has ruined our cities and hill-stations.' Shourie particularly regrets the passing of 'a certain reticence and a certain tentativeness' which were peculiarly British and exemplified for him, not by 'the imperial certainties' of the Raj, but by the academic atmosphere of British universities. 'That tentativeness,' he complains, 'which is very valuable, and was also the great feature of a tradition like Hinduism, will certainly be swamped by mere Americanisms.'

In colonial times, there were noticeable differences between the kind of westernisation that took place in the south, rooted in traditional Hinduism, and the more hybrid, northern provinces. Today the distinction is between the older, colonial middle-class, with its discreet and selective adaptation of Western ways, and the more imitative and tasteless westernisation of the *nouveau riche*, often from lower middle-class, vernacular backgrounds, who are climbing the ladder of upward mobility. The latter, ironically, are sometimes the most avid consumers of a colonial ritual which once completely excluded them. They are the new Anglo-Indians, desperately seeking, like their racially hybrid predecessors during the Raj, a social acceptance denied them by material success alone.

Probably the most extreme example of their snobbery is the Madras Club, till the late 1950s an exclusive European preserve, where no Indian could set foot, even as a guest. By the time the dwindling number of Europeans in Madras forced the club to open its doors to Indians, most of the city's older families had little interest in joining. A Cambridge-educated aristocrat like Govind Swaminathan, former Advocate-General of Madras, says that he can never forget the time when he would have been refused entry because of the colour of his skin. But such pride carries little weight with the younger, urban professionals who now run the club.

Its present chairman, Dr Krishna Rau, is in his forties and heads the city's most exclusive private hospital, the Willingdon Nursing Home, founded by a former vicereine. He waxes eloquent about the importance of maintaining British standards, whether in clubs or hospitals. He is particularly proud of the club's strict Western dress code, which fetishises the wearing of shoes and socks instead of sandals. 'A certain amount of relaxation,' he explains, 'leads to a situation where there is no point of return. Here we meet people who are all from the cream of society. . . . If you are walking through the club to the swimming pool, you can go in swimming trunks, which is absolutely nothing. So you can come in a swimming dress, and you'll be permitted to get into the club; but you may not come in Indian dress.'

Such crude snobbery is everywhere, from the arts to government, in the new India. One can see it in the Americanised film culture that is the opium of the masses, or in more genteel adaptations of West End and Broadway hits for the Indian stage. Politically, it is expressed in the obeisance of semi-literate, political mafiosi to a ruling dynasty represented by one of India's most westernised and patrician families. 'We are the decoration for the gentlemen who are really manipulating the political machine,' says Romesh Thapar about the westernised upper class to which he belongs. 'They introduce us in order to gain respectability. The dynasty that they set up knows less about the country than even I; but it is a vested interest of the gangsters who've got into politics. They need a dynasty as the godhead to which everybody bows.'

According to Thapar, Prime Minister Rajiv Gandhi and his coterie of Oxbridge-educated advisers are so far removed from an understanding of the real India that they fall back on the old law-and-order approach to government, and on tactics of divide and rule, which perpetuate a new colonial domination of India's rural masses by its urban élites.

All the development which has taken place in India has increased the gulf between rich and poor. Who are the urban and rural rich? There would be about 10 million people who really have surplus; and supporting them are these enormous urban centres with all kinds of luxuries and five-star culture. The policies are meant to support this sort of five-star culture, because this is how the élite of India wants to present itself to the world. But people in the rural areas, one hour out of Delhi, are living another life.

If you take the statistics, only some 4 million people, in a country of 750 millions, are eligible to pay tax. But you have 350 million people below the poverty line, after 38 years of development; and this poverty base will be 500 million people by the year 2000. But the attempt is to manage through manipulation, through moving one community this way, another community that way – divide and rule, it remains the same. We still function in that way, of looking at the opposition and trying to divide it, instead of trying to understand the problems of each region and integrating them into a national policy. The colonial masters were at least more sensitive about regional variations, because they had to rule with a handful of men, and they knew they couldn't play this game in a foolish way.

The new colonialism, according to Thapar, is as hierarchical and status-conscious as the old, despite its socialist rhetoric.

One of the most terrible mutations that took place in India was that the caste system of the Hindus was married to the class system of the British. This led literally to looking down on the person who was below you and keeping your distance. You can go to Malaya, which was occupied by the British, and your taxi-driver will get out, shake your hand and say: 'Have a good day!' No taxi-driver would dare do that in India, because it would be considered uppity. That's the difference.

Despite their arrogance towards those they consider their inferiors, India's rulers themselves suffer from what many would regard as a colonial inferiority complex in relation to Western expertise. Tara Ali Baig, who has been active in various social welfare projects, describes how this has distorted development priorities.

I discovered to my horror that people who were going abroad for training were being trained in the problems of the West and coming back as experts to give us all the wrong advice. Take our first Five-Year Plan in 1952. The experts on social welfare, who had come back from abroad, concentrated on juvenile delinquency, psychiatric treatment and child-care centres, when in actual fact what we needed were nutrition, preventative health care and investment in the child. These are things that have only now been recognised in this seventh Five-Year Plan. So we could have saved a lot of time had we not had this expertise.

Although official rhetoric puts far more emphasis on rural development than the British ever did, the urban bias continues to be reflected in the over-centralised structure and planning of most development programmes. Mehra Masani cites broadcasting as an example.

The government should be concentrating on public service television for underprivileged people, who would be viewing programmes on community sets. But such a development is not possible so long as government is so totally concerned with the urban vote; they are the people who bring the pressure for the kind of programmes that television gives us now. What I would like in radio is local stations servicing a radius of maybe twenty or at the most forty miles, where the idiom and the interests reflected would be entirely local. One of the reasons why our rural programmes have not had the impact they should is because they come from a regional centre miles and miles away from the farmer, and he feels that these people just talk a lot of academic blah-blah about what fertilisers and pesticides to use. He wants an example nearer home.

If there is a new urban colonialism today, then its palaces are undoubtedly the garish five-star hotels and luxury apartment blocks which have sprung from the ashes of past colonial elegance. The main urban centres of the British Raj remain the hub of economic and cultural life in modern India; but, in most cases, the combined onslaught of the new rich and the rural poor has changed their landscapes beyond recognition. The rural masses whom the Raj neglected have wreaked a retrospective revenge. They have invaded the great cities of British India in search of food and work and set up their teeming shanty-towns amid the dilapidated Victorian-Gothic monuments that were once the pride of empire. Their main rivals have been unscrupulous property speculators, whose jerry-built, high-rise blocks have crushed any attempt at urban planning. Cusrow Irani, who came to live in Calcutta in 1949, mourns the disappearance of the once gracious city he knew.

Calcutta has been a great city in the past, with great amenities, and these have disappeared. Statistically, the city is not fit for human habitation – the pollution level is unacceptably high, housing is pathetic, public transport is almost non-existent, telephones work less here than in other cities.

It's much more crowded now than it used to be, and certain landmarks have disappeared. One of the finest restaurants in the whole country, Firpo's, has become a market – a rabbit-warren of little shops overrun by hawkers. There were none of these awful eyesores on Chowringhee, the main thoroughfare. The Maidan was an expanse of greenery with lovely trees, which have been cut down. The buildings look far more dilapidated than before, and some of the better ones have been pulled down by developers. The Bengal Club, for instance, was a magnificent building, with beautiful marble staircases. It had four cooks who made nothing but omelettes all day long and wouldn't soil their hands doing anything else. I don't know many clubs in the world which can afford the luxury of four cooks who only make omelettes. But that sort of thing carried on for too long, the losses mounted, and the club building had to be sold.

There used to be a certain leisurely pace about life in Calcutta. You had time to go home after work, have a bath, change into your dinner-jacket, then go out to a concert, and on to dinner with a splendidly lit table. The ambience was different. Life is more rushed now: it takes you five or six times as long to get home from your place of work. Lunching out has become thoroughly unfashionable now, because it is impractical; you would waste three hours for even a hurried meal, because the transport is so bad.

In the old days, the Calcutta streets were regularly washed. I remember, when I was setting out to go to office, you had to be very careful if you were leaving early, because you would be showered with water by the road-cleaners. The roads used to be washed and then brushed and cleaned. And in the evenings, people would run up and down the streets lighting up the gas-lamps and then come back and turn them off in the morning. Now there is no question of any washing of streets; the streets are washed for three or four months of the year when the monsoon rains come down. As for street lights, if the power supply is on, which it very often isn't, nobody bothers to switch them off; so you have the spectacle of electric lights blazing away at nine in the morning in bright sunshine.

Ironically, the urban decay and poverty of which the élite complain are the price of urban economic domination and the growing rural unemployment it creates. Irani and most other urban conservationists agree that the main cause of urban overcrowding has been the waves of rural migration into the cities. This, they argue, could have been avoided by a policy of decentralised growth, based on smaller, village-based industrial and agricultural projects, instead of 'the expensive new temples' of heavy industry.

The breakdown of urban services is also closely linked to the notorious corruption of municipal politics. Local government was the sphere in which British India first introduced representative institutions; and the calibre of Indian city fathers and the quality of their debates was once said to have rivalled those of the best-run British boroughs. But according to M. R. Masani, a former Mayor of Bombay, the political and economic compulsions of more recent urbanisation have brought a collapse of municipal standards.

When I was Mayor, from 1943 to '44, we were very proud of Bombay. We had a coat of arms with the motto, *Urbs Prima in Indis*, 'The First City in India', and we thought we were. At that time, municipal elections were not run by political parties; and this meant that, in each of the wards, the local citizen was able to choose between one man and another on the strength of their education, their equipment and their political track-record. Today the political parties have hogged municipal elections, and people are elected without reference to their own qualifications. People say you can even elect a lamp-post if he's a Congress candidate; and now we have too many lamp-posts and not enough of the kind of people who made Bombay what it was by being strong civic leaders. The Mayor of Bombay was once upon a time a very eminent citizen; but he's now anyone who can get the majority party to vote him in.

When I was Mayor, I used to go and visit the working-class area; and in my time, that was considered a slum. But now those very working-class dwellings are not slums at all, but considered quite respectable. The slums of today are little huts on marshy land, which are swamped by the monsoon water and have terribly unhygienic conditions. So the slum of 1943 is now a very respectable dwelling for the worker, and that shows the deterioration in housing standards.

Despite such comparisons, few Indians today, whether they live in five-star luxury or fetid slums, feel any nostalgia for British rule. What many survivors of the Raj do miss is the idealism and sincerity of their own past. For all its humiliations, they remember the alien presence as a challenge which often brought out the best in themselves. At its best, the Western impact provoked Indian scholars and reformers to rediscover their own heritage and assimilate other cultures in a spirit of enquiry very different from the imitative westernisation of today. Even at its worst, foreign rule imposed on Indians a solidarity of resistance that left little room for more selfish concerns. The poet Harindranath Chattopadhyaya retains at the age of 88 much of the youthful optimism with which he set out as a student to discover Edwardian England. But according to him, the new India has much to learn from the lost dreams of its colonial elders.

We were a simpler generation, a deeper and more honest generation, a most beautiful give-and-take generation who had faith in each other; and we could trust people. When we bought something worth thousands, we did not need to ask for receipts. But now I don't think you can trust people very much. I see that it's all progressing in the modern sense of the term; we are doing fine things, and structures are being built. But, at the same time, I feel that we are still not unshackled. I wish that our women could walk the streets without any fear, that we could do beautiful things without interference. But we can't today, because there are no opportunities given. This is not an age when your dreams mean anything to you; and unless you have dreams and dreamers, you can't have independence.

SELECT BIBLIOGRAPHY

David, Kingsley: *The Population of India and Pakistan*. Princeton University Press, New Jersey, 1951.

Dutt, B. C.: *Mutiny of the Innocents*. Sindhu Publications, Bombay, 1971.

Edwardes, Michael: *Raj*. Pan, London, 1967.

Griffiths, Sir Percival: *The British Impact on India*. Macdonald, London, 1952.

Hiro, Dilip: *Inside India Today*. Routledge and Kegan Paul, London, 1976.

Masani, R. P.: *Britain in India*. Oxford University Press, Oxford, 1960.

Misra, B. B.: *The Indian Middle Classes*. Oxford University Press, Oxford, 1961.

Morris, James: *Pax Britannica*. Penguin, London, 1984.
Farewell the Trumpets. Penguin, London, 1984.

Spear, Percival: *A History of India, Volume II*. Penguin, London, 1985.
The Oxford History of Modern India. Clarendon Press, Oxford, 1965.

Thapar, Romila: *A History of India, Volume I*. Penguin, London, 1966.

Thompson, Edward, and Garratt, G. T.: *Rise and Fulfilment of British Rule in India*. Macmillan, London, 1934.

Woodruff, Philip: *The Men Who Ruled India: The Founders*. Jonathan Cape, London, 1963.
The Men Who Ruled India: The Guardians. Jonathan Cape, London, 1963.

Picture Credits

BARNABY'S PICTURE LIBRARY steelworks, page 64; BBC HULTON PICTURE LIBRARY Lord Clive, page 59, cartoon, page 61, traders, page 65, clubs, both page 66, Besant, page 101, police, page 105; BRITISH LIBRARY (INDIA OFFICE LIBRARY) revenue officers, page 59, judicial officers, page 60, battle, page 62, sailors, page 63, entertainment, page 65, school cricket, page 102; COUNCIL FOR WORLD MISSION Christian converts, both page 100; IMPERIAL WAR MUSEUM army officer, page 63; MANSELL COLLECTION Tagore, page 101; PHOTO SOURCE race meeting, page 99, Gandhi, page 104, Nehru and Bose, page 104; POPPERFOTO high court, pages 60–1, sepoys, page 62, banquet, page 99, team, page 102, colleges, both page 103, the Alis, page 104, demonstration, page 105, legislature, page 106; SONDEEP SHANKAR Beating Retreat, page 106; TATA LTD. house, portrait, both page 64.